T0114756

EARS
BUT CAN'T HEAR

How the Inability to Hear Changes the Way We See the World

SAM WITTKE

WestBow Press books may be ordered through booksellers or by contacting:

WestBow Press
A Division of Thomas Nelson & Zondervan
1663 Liberty Drive
Bloomington, IN 47403
www.westbowpress.com
844-714-3454

ISBN: 978-1-6642-6715-2 (sc)
ISBN: 978-1-6642-6714-5 (e)

Print information available on the last page.

WestBow Press rev. date: 05/16/2022

INTRODUCTION

One of the symptoms of a society that suffers from a spiritual dilemma is that it is always going and never stopping. Restlessness and mania, psychologically, shows a problem with a person's mind, whether that problem is depression or addiction or something else. "Sociologically," then, wouldn't these conditions indicate the same problem with peoples' minds—and if this problem, whether pertaining to individuals or the societies that they inhabit, is continuously duplicating itself from age to age, is it wise to consider the problem to be a new problem which must be overcome through sheer innovation? Has the high octane, secular, and relativistic new era come into the world to save us from the world, or do these things only remind us of what the teacher already said was present thousands of years ago in his time and the times before him?

In modern thought, we have forfeited the ancient accumulated knowledge to an aerial bombardment of intellectual ideas that come from every which way. Ironically this new knowledge cannot function without the foundation of the old. Moreover, interpreting the new age cannot be done without the wisdom of old age. The only way forward, as a society, is to learn once more that it is acceptable to reject things again. In fact a person cannot live in adherence to a moral law that is constantly accepting everything—such a confusing law is a thousand times more legalistic and condemning than any law it has already overthrown for being too rigid. After all, doesn't acceptance of many laws and worldviews by its very nature mean that one also condemns what those laws and worldviews condemn? But when we reject certain untrue things, do we not free ourselves to accept what's true? When we reject the good, we leave an opening for evil. When we reject evil, we leave an opening for good.

The new law is meant to create so much noise that it ends up deafening everything around it, including the church. Constant noise has replaced the truth. In the new age, total liberty has proven to be a bondage far more constraining and difficult to emerge from than anything that has arisen before it.

It is wise for the church to interpret the times, or at least try to. The inability to interpret the times, of which I am far too often unable to do, shows *not* that we are standing in the midst of times that do not need to be interpreted because they somehow transcend yesterday's more ancient and outdated times, but that we are so deeply entrenched in these modern times that we cannot objectively weigh and evaluate them. These modern times fit the pattern of many times that came before. But we are unable to recognize them as times at all. Instead we see them as something new, even eternal. A recognition of some basic signs of the times is liberating in how simple it is, but terrifying in its implications for people's various wants and desires. So this recognition is often avoided.

It's hard to ignore the most basic pattern of scripture, especially when scripture is read over the widening backdrop of the new age. A warning to the new age church of which I am a part is necessary, because of this basic pattern. I do not reference the church *as a building* in which we gather to hear, but the gathering of the only people that ought to be gathered. The church should have one body, not many. We should have one set of ears, one pair of hands, one mind, one set of lips, two eyes, and one beating heart. Instead, so many are becoming double minded.

Reading scripture in the midst of the new age is incredibly powerful. By restricting us from one type of fleeting liberty, the Lord opens us to another, even more emancipating liberty. Living a life of faith has become taboo in any other sense than the one faith considered acceptable in the eyes of the world. A faith in anything other than self-governed-law is rejected by the prince of this world.

My warning for the church comes not from an attitude of resentment for the church, or for my peers within the church, but from resemblances between the apostolic warnings to the early church and modern church practices. We have become divided along so many religious, legal, political, cultural and denominational lines that it is becoming impossible to tell what's what and who's who. Gnosticism is reemerging. New Ageism (to be distinguished from "the new age" I've spoken about which is the modern epoch) which includes many alternative religious practices including witchcraft, worship of false gods, and moral relativism is entering many churches. The church is becoming largely indifferent to the shedding of innocent blood. Many churches don't even see the Bible as divinely inspired anymore, but mostly allegory. Many churches use the gospel as a platform for profit. Still others worship angels, become lukewarm, or integrate political or cultural agendas into doctrine.

There are question marks surrounding every word in scripture, from beginning to end. Everything in scripture becomes debatable on a spectrum that ranges from inauthentic to inerrant. The legality of certain actions, or words, or ideas about theology are cast into question, and what constitutes a sin is shrouded in mystery because of this new division. Some see street preaching or voting republican as sinful, and think there's nothing wrong with homosexuality or abortion. Others think demons inhabit DVDs and CDs. Cultural ideals that have long contradicted the church and the teachings of Christ, often with heightened distain, are making their way through church doors and to the altar. When the apostles saw division in the earliest church, although some divisions emerged from a question of which teacher to follow, they warned against it, especially when demonic practices manifested. Today such aberrations have become the norm rather than the exception. Many teachers who often carry the most authority have become much more diluted in their knowledge of the truth by trying to supplement the gospel with hollow and deceptive philosophies like progressivism and Gnosticism to gain knowledge. Others have put themselves under other strange new forms of legalism, sometimes in a knee jerk reaction to the dangers of progressive Christianity.

This book was not meant to be a warning to the church. But in the American church we should acknowledge that the configurations that were alive in the world in the past are no less alive today. They may be pressing closer than ever. The books of Jude, 2 Peter, and Revelation all speak of certain teachings making their way into the church. But they were not new teachings. They were present at Moses's time, and even dated back to Cain. These teachings involve elements like consulting false gods (demons), Spiritism, sexual immorality, worldly ambition in the church, and false prophecy. This means that when we see similar elements modernly corrupt the church, we should not make any differentiation between them and the most ancient sins, we should see them as directly rebellious to God, and we should acknowledge that real demonic powers are likely behind them.

When the church accepts even a small part of the world pattern as true even as it contradicts the pattern Christ modeled, we become blind to the sight of the world pattern and deaf to its sounds. Do we really need Paul to make a trip from heaven to warn us about this again? Every book in scripture spends a good deal of time explaining sin, warning against it and demonstrating its corresponding forms. It's not as if sin's any less of a threat today. Perhaps it is just another futile suggestion of mine, as no solid interpretation can seem to be presently grasped without a rein of fiery contradictions. But only a realization of the condition will lead to a search for the cure. To what degree is the presence of this condition is alive in the church today? Did we overcome Baalam's error and Korah's rebellion? If not, how may we identify their expressions presently?

After the Lord led Israel out of their bondage, they forgot their God and His prophet and formed a bronze image of a calf. They became convinced that this image was the god that led them from Israel, even though they fabricated it in a moment of spiritual folly. The real God was simply taking too long to show up for them in the wilderness so they forsook Him, and traded Him for a god of the gaps—a god of the imagination. It was not that God was shouting at them and they became deaf because of it. Their ability to hear was stifled by the volume of their own voices, and their own theological interpretations of who or what God may be. Their ability to see the invisible God was traded for the immediate reward of a visible idol. Fortunately God was patient with them, as He is patient with us.

THE BREATH OF LIFE

Breathing is the most immediate physical necessity and the only corporeal need that is invisible. So in a way, the foundation of life itself, which distinguishes living from nonliving and conscious from unconscious, is itself a testament to the physical and the visible being secondary to and dependent on the spiritual and invisible, that the body is linked to the spirit. When we enter into the world, the first thing we need is air to breathe, and when we leave the world the last thing that we give up is our breath, which comes out from our lungs. Breath is forgotten and taken for granted, and so life is often taken for granted. We take life for granted when we forget that we were meant to be spiritual creatures. We forsake the spiritual aspect of our being when we turn from God. So for any person, the closest they can come to what they perceive to be God, apart from God, is by acknowledging breath, for breath signifies the invisible connection between all living things. The loss of breath signifies death.

As the air is to our lungs, so Christ is to our spirit. He surrendered His Spirit to God along with the last breath from His body so that many would be saved by His Spirit and His breath. That our breath leaves our body on its own and returns on its own is a gift from God in itself. The air itself shows that the hope of life is not in our own ability to breathe, it is in the one who gives our breath to us and later takes our breath away. Our hope in the Spirit is not in our ability to control the Spirit, but to allow Him to run His course like the wind. Adam was formed, and then he was given the breath of life. The Christian is saved, and then is given the life of the Spirit. We must be born again, not have a change of mind or heart (although our mind and heart will be changed along with our knowledge and desire). So to know Christ is not to abandon our bodies, or the world for that matter, but to know what is between God and man—Spirit—even as we know what is between heaven and earth—wind. Christ made it possible to know God and to love the world like God, yet to be invisible to the world while always present within the world, shaping the world like wind.

THE FOUNDATION OF ARROGANCE

Arrogance comes from a made up mind, a mind that has made itself up by building itself out of nothing. Arrogance occurs when the created becomes the creator, and the creator becomes the created. We are all living as versions of ourselves, versions of the intended form, the selfless self—for the best version of the self is the form which did not intend itself.

The condition that one may call arrogance or pride is a condition that begins in the ears, then moves to the eyes, then to the hands, and corrupts the whole body. For first Adam and Eve heard the lie from the serpent, then they saw that the fruit was good and pleasing to the eye, and then they reached with their hand to grab it, eat it, and digest it. The sin of pride must manifest as a thought before it turns to a vision—and it must be seen before it is acted upon. The actions of the body follow the thoughts of the mind. The thoughts of a mind must conform to a teaching which is already there, a teaching that is already seen and has already been acted upon by another person or angel.

The pride of life is a visual extension of the first thoughts of a man being separated from his creator. The eye is no longer a created thing in what it sees, alive in its realization of pure dependence on God, but a fading creation of a new type of creature that realizes its own nakedness and hides. The eye enters into the captivity of seeing reality initially through the lens of its own corruption, and no longer through unalloyed unity with God. As soon as thought is changed to be something other than what it was designed for, vision becomes something other than what it was meant to be as well. Action, the habits that repeated actions lead to, and the movements of all others who follow these actions, all conform to this vision as well. This prolonged series of individual and communal configurations forms what Christians have nicknamed "the pattern of this world." So the most visible pattern of the world begins within the hidden intentions of the heart. This binary nature of pride is the problem of pride which shrouds it as it spreads through the world either in the form of unconscious sins or great mounting skyscrapers. Human pride creates another world altogether to stand up defiantly against reality—not a world created for man, but a world created by man. This would-be creation is the "world pattern" which we have seen concurrently building itself up and then collapsing in on itself, only to try and rebuild itself again through history.

The intent of our own vision is to recreate everything in the image of what comes before our eyes. By refashioning what has already been fashioned in the hands of the creator who is naturally seated above man, man eliminates the need for the one who transcends him and creates things on his own, without the knowledge of his own lower status of creature. However, because man can no longer see what is unseen because he is blinded by his pride, and can no longer hear or speak to the one he has rejected, the things he creates can only be reproductions of what are likewise deaf, mute, and blind figurines of what has fallen from the grace and truth which were once intended.

God, by the work of His hands, showed us what the work of our hands could be—only if we maintained the ability to hear and understand and fear Him. It was an existence within the strictures of paradise. Rebellion rejected those boundaries and broke through them. God promised that if, in our search for hidden knowledge, we forsook his voice and sacrificed our knowledge and fear of Him, we would enter into spiritual death. The body would be soon to follow. The search for a life apart from the life we'd been given would be to surgically remove life from its definition as gift, redefining it as something we've earned.

As we live life, each person in turn is *bound to fall* into this thought, the thought's ensuing vision, its vision's pattern of action, and step out into the world that these consequential patterns resulted in. Every man and woman will suffer the condition of closing our ears to what is true. They will come to the same conclusion as Eve and Pilot: there can be no truth apart from what one makes of it. Every man and woman will cause suffering and will suffer at the hands of others who are also under this condition. Arrogance makes the world *by* man only a cultivation of his own vision of it apart from what the world actually is. This image is an aberration of heaven. It draws nearer to a man's heart as he strolls steadily towards death because of his suppression of the truth. Man thinks it's his job to bring about the restoration of Eden. And he's right, partly.

So far as we know, death is the one thing that is more popular than life. Each person knows about and believes in the lie of death because he or she does not recognize the truth of life. Jesus Christ confirmed through His death and resurrection that death is the lie and that life is the truth. It was difficult to shake His disciples free from the belief that His death was final, even after His resurrection. When God promised death as a result of disobedience, He did not promise immediate physical execution as a punishment for a crime, but a spiritual poison and to replace the invisible truth with a visible myth that would come once the eyes that were never intended to be opened were opened. Versions of this myth take form in every generation. The truth is that life is paramount to death, as light overcomes darkness at the dawn. The myth is that death is the only thing certain to humanity—that even life is indefinite compared to its cessation. The world indoctrinates a man with the finality of death as well as idolatrous remedies to suspend death throughout the time he spends in it.

The idol represents the first time that the mind of man drifted from the truth and fastened itself onto something foreign to the reality God intended. The idolater, in a spiritual sense, has ears but cannot hear, eyes but cannot see, a mouth but cannot speak. Mind becomes a form created in its own image, only learning what a man can learn once he has become as a god. We want to imitate God in the exact opposite way He intended us to—as our own designers and saviors at the pinnacle of knowledge and existence. We scramble to steal his attributes. Then we are free to design our own gods fashioned after our own nature and our own perspective of nature—bronze calves and clay statuettes of ourselves. This freedom of design comes from the rejection of the *imago dei* design. We thought this design kept us in bondage. The definitive design from the Word spells imprisonment in the mind of sinful man. The world as we see it today and the voices we hear in it and the things we make out of it are a result of our escape from this "prison," the prison of reality, wherein our freedom truly once was pure, uncorrupted by sin and death. True freedom is as enigmatic as the meaning of life.

We have not only redefined everything, we have defined it backwards. Rather than defining life from life, we redefine life in reverse from death. So the mind of sinful man becomes death. The sinful mind was also *conceived* at the moment of our corporate death. Consider the broad parallel of modern naturalism. We technically came from nothing and created ourselves via evolution, and after we live for a time as organisms, we will return back to nothing. Everything is physically fixed and certain, so nothing spiritually is, which is why there are so many contradicting spiritual explanations that shoot off from naturalism. We are now held in the bondage of an absolute certainty of nothing, because we thought we had attained an absolute certainty of everything following the intellectual abandonment of God. Modern naturalism is the closest philosophy to the promise of the curse of the fall. We come from dust, one cell. Our cells grow and multiply as we develop. Then they peak, slowly degenerate, and decompose at our death. We return to physical dust. During this time we are destined to toil and struggle to survive. Darwinian naturalism is so compelling because it is the most accurate philosophical explanation of physical existence which followed man's separation from spiritual existence.

Nothing, in the mind of man apart from God, is the creator of everything. So the man who professes to know everything about everything also inadvertently admits to knowing nothing about anything. A degeneration of spiritual understanding was meant for us at the departure from the foundation of understanding structured on the fear of the Lord. If our knowledge begins in a humble recognition of our own identity as fallible, dependent creatures, we admit to knowing nothing about ourselves aside from that true nature. So we know more about ourselves than everyone else. Rather than starting from the knowledge of everything and then degenerating back to intellectual dust, we begin by knowing nothing but the foundation God has laid and from there we develop or evolve into the true intended form of God's imaging in us. The humble recognition to knowing nothing but to fear God and keep His commandments is the beginning of the path to true understanding, as Wisdom once told. This was the conclusion to the paradox of life. This path was narrow from beginning to end.

Intellectual humility is the singularity to the universe of true thoughtfulness. Solomon *asked* God for wisdom, knowing he didn't have it. The apostles were praying for God's direction when the Holy Spirit descended upon them. Nebuchadnezzar was given the mind of a beast *first* in order to regain his true mind seven years later, which began with a recognition of God's sovereignty. Paul had to be made blind *so that* the scales would later fall from his eyes.

There can be no light without the one who said, "Let there be light" (Genesis 1:3) and no life without the one in whose life was the light of mankind. Therefore both light and life signify beginning and beginner, not randomness or an arbitrary light of life. They also signify righteousness, what is right, just as righteousness is like the first gleam of dawn, shining brighter and brighter until the noonday sun. The ones who are on the side of truth see the light of the truth and listen to the words of the one who brings light into life through the light that is in the truth. The ones who *choose* the life of darkness ask "what is truth," even as they put truth on trial to condemn it so that they may remain in their darkness. Truth becomes a public spectacle to be mocked and derided. Those who live only in the "here and now" claim also to know everything about the "there and then." But they are hopelessly lost in the present until they acknowledge the hope of the Alpha and Omega, the only hope who stands forever outside time, with one foot at the beginning and one foot at the end. The whole earth is His footstool.

The certainty of the beginning and the end in the eyes of the lost creature is only what has been settled in its scientific discovery as what cannot by nature be found, because it is shrouded in darkness. We find ourselves living in the eternal paradox that knowledge without God leads to, regardless of the various personal aspirations and pleasures, monumental technological achievements, vast libraries of infinite information, and persuasive modern mythologies that arise within this paradox. Everything that is certain becomes uncertain. So regenerative faith is not in the certainties of this world which can appear to stand so strong right before they crumble into dust and ashes.

THE WORDS AND WAYS OF THE WORLD

There were many times when Jesus closed His message with the words "He who has ears to hear let him hear" (Matthew 11:15). The hearers are the ones Jesus is specifically addressing. His message is for those who have retained the ability to listen or who want to listen, not for those who are of the world, and can only hear from the world, those who only want to hear from the world. Those who are of the world have reformed their ways to align with the words that the world speaks. These ways become deeply entrenched roads within the world system. They are set on paths that have already been tread throughout the ages. So it is difficult to hear anything of God or of heaven because the words of God and of heaven show a path to a different life, the life which they have not learned to love yet. Loving this new life merits hating one's old life. The call to new life can only be heard by those who have ears that are open to a new voice.

The path that the Lord calls us to is narrow and difficult to recognize at all when the wide and easily recognizable road that we have chosen is all we know. The wide road becomes not only the only thing we know, but the only thing we ever want to know. This is our way, and it is the inescapable way of the world. The words of a person stem from their heart, whether their heart condition is formed by the promise or the curse. The words that one chooses tell others of the path they've chosen and will continue to choose. If the words one speaks have deceit and pride, which are symptoms of the curse, they will build a false view of the world to rival God's view of the world. They think this view is a new building, but it is only another brick. If the words one speaks are true, they will cause others to see things as they are, where the world and the heavens are viewed as creation. Apart from the creator, the creation's fabric frays at the edges. Eventually its structure crumbles altogether. The one who has hardened their heart, who has ears but cannot hear and eyes but cannot see, sees the world and the heavens as something other than what they are. The quest for a theory of everything begins with a faulty observation of everything.

The one who has robbed God of His authorship is destined to become the new author of all that is, at least for the time being in his own mind. No matter how foolish this desire is, when it is fueled by pride and deceit it is impossible to tell the person otherwise. The world came to the same conclusions long ago. It affirms the person who is his own god in his decision to follow his own law.

The heavens and earth become a perversion of the new heaven and new earth under the condition. Countless things are recreated godlessly as quickly as they can be reinterpreted as godless. The earth and the heavens become self-sustaining when the words of a person tell them that they are. And who is to tell them otherwise in a world that will outlive us? They have already given their ears to the altar of that world.

The new heavens and earth of the worldly pattern are shrouded in darkness and doubt as they must be with nothing as their creator. The new earth has a law of self-governance and relative truth as it must have with rulers who will only hear what their itching ears want to hear. Humans become as darkened gods, inbred by the immutable darkness and nothingness of our own perceived divine essence. We are germs on a tennis ball who think we govern the tennis court. When our eyes were opened to god-like-ness, our ears were closed to godliness. When we followed the devil, we became lost in the darkness and separated from peace, destined to move to the far reaches of the earth in confusion. We went to the place we thought our thirst would be fulfilled, but at the edge of the water we became trapped by awe of our own reflection.

Somehow—even as one is both as-god and as-nothing in an existence of overwhelming darkness and emptiness—they lie to themselves and others until the whole world believes that we are the guiding light for it, here to rewrite the definition of existence and show the way to heaven. So every man creates his own law of condemnation and holds the expectation of his law over the whole world. To be both nothing and everything, light and darkness, good and evil, as well as judge of the world at all times is enough to drive a man mad with delusions of being God, or to suicide with delusions of being nothing. This is the condition of the new divine man, who is also hiding the shame of his own nakedness and nothingness.

What would a world look like in such a confused state? It would look like many loudly proclaiming their own mastery over everything and silently contemplating their own insignificance and understanding of nothing. Men and women everywhere would be at one moment considering personal transcendence and at another moment considering biological decomposition. Human excellence would be at once unquestionable and untenable. There would be great towers into the sky next to wide pits reaching into the earth. Those places are where the new collective consciousness always is, reaching toward the heavens and descending into the pit, by way of the spiritual equivalent of gravity—pride. Ears keep listening for the voice of the mute idols they have made. These idols stretch a man farther than he is meant to be stretched, giving him hope where there is none, and then condemning him. Idolatry is a giant cosmic scam.

Human achievement no longer emerges from a familial or communal bond, but out of selfish competitiveness and bitter envy. When one builds everything out of nothing, they can get nothing out of anything, and so everything becomes nothing. The quest for everything under the sun becomes meaningless, as the great teacher once said. The new man is seeking his own deity and glory. When he is closest to finding it, all of the sudden he cannot escape his own purposelessness. The laws of the world will always lead a man to sleep no matter how much he wants to stay awake. The truth of God will waken him no matter how much he wants to stay asleep.

There are many roads in the world today, winding between civilizations and neighborhoods. There are infinite directions one can take—and there is no telling a person which way he or she ought to go. The farther a person drives along on a road, the less likely they are to turn around when they are told that they are going the wrong way, or even to stop and ask for directions. The road they are on has a promised destination, but it is a promise that has come from nothing higher than the driver himself. The words we whisper to ourselves in the morning are enough to keep us on this road, enough to tell us that the destination we have imagined is still there—if it ever even was there at all.

The dreams and visions of a person can be at once their greatest gift and their greatest curse, for there is no subduing a false dream or vision which has been interpreted as true. There is no stopping the forward movement of a man or a woman when the end they desire has already been promised by words written long ago by the world's ways. The person, lost and stumbling, keeps going as their heart leads them—and their heart is not in disagreement with the hearts of others. The many achievements of human folly reveal themselves along the timeline, masquerading as wise things. Before we know it we stand in the midst of a culture as blind, deaf, and dumb as the idols it created, compelled by God to turn around and start walking towards him, but convinced in the stubbornness of our own foolish hearts that the path we have set out on is the true path, the path to the one and only god we've dreamt up. It is only the path to self-worship, which will lead to torment eternal, the compounded and unending world pattern and the undying desperation of the flesh that multiplies suffering. We will be at once constantly torn apart to become as nothing, even as we are trying to rebuild ourselves back up into everything. Eternal punishment may be something like immortally diseased servitude to everyone's unresolvable even demonic desires. It is also a real place.

This is the curse of the self when our eyes are opened to the wide way of the world which has been told to us by the prideful one. We are cursed to destroy ourselves and destroy others as quickly as we believe that we can build ourselves up and build up others. This is why we are told by Christ that we cannot love our own life and at the same time keep it. For this life that we love is not the life God created for us, but the life we have built for ourselves out of our own ambition. Therefore what we desire—restoration, redemption, salvation, heaven, reconciliation, victory and hope—is traded for manufactured versions in order to keep going on this road. However, these principles were given to a person to help them understand that they are great mysteries, too great for mankind simply to have imagined over and over again on its own. The fact that we all yearn for them and fall short of them shows their absolute and transcendent nature.

There is much more than the self, even the collective self. Manufactured ideals that strive to fit the true ones can be indicators and warning signs that a person is on the wrong path when what they believe turns out not to hold strong in the midst of true pain and suffering quite like it was supposed to, even if the religion offered temporary vainglory and pleasure.

God tells us that we are not capable of building the way to the saving of the world merely by our own words. For our words are perceived to be the foundation for our lives and are faulty, idle and skewed. Our lives walk in the wrong direction, the same direction as our words, as a law of human nature. It is impossible to cure ourselves of our spiritual blindness. Mankind has built the new way, rewritten the new truth, and redefined the new life. There is no cure found within the new world for the old disease, for the new world has been built to avoid the cure for the disease in order to keep us suffering from it.

TWO DIFFERENT GIFTS

The gift of life was always the gift of God. Existence itself was a gift to man and woman. It was impossible to achieve by their own volition. How can you achieve what you already are? When the true gift of being was forsaken for idol worship and lust for power, people's idea of what a gift was shifted. There was no more gift of God, but only the wages of iniquity.

God spent a week writing the proof of our gift in the heavens and earth for all to see as long as we drew breath. He also gave us full knowledge of the gift in paradise, when our wills were so well aligned with his. But it was our innate freedom which allowed us to shift the intention of the will from God, deviating from His path and onto our own. At first, the path away from God was uncharted territory. Now it has been well travelled. It is the path leading back towards God that is far less recognizable.

The stunning truth about God's gift to us was that it included everything, and excluded nothing—our definitions of "everything" and "nothing" were vulnerable to attack. United with Him in His nature, humanity was allowed true freedom and simple access to the greatest mysteries a man can imagine today. Humanity was truly blessed in this early condition, truly blessed in true freedom within the condition's designation which was our design. We all know the story. Some know it as untrue even in the church. Others recognize it as a longsuffering explanation of the human condition. One chapter still stands unrivaled by mountains of books written by the wisdom of the world to show why things are the way they are. The story is an account of how mankind traded the gift for a lie long ago, thinking the gift was the lie and the lie was the gift.

No matter how far a person stands removed from the time of the first sin, they still stand at the very beginning of it in each and every moment, facing the ancient choice. We have the freedom to choose. It was implicit in the gift. This means the freedom to choose the lie was a part of the gift, but it doesn't mean the lie was the gift or intended in the gift. The more we become accustomed to choosing one thing instead of another, the less likely we are to choose the other thing. Addiction is a worldly example. What's unfamiliar, sobriety, threatens to take the gift that we chose away, even when the gift is not a gift at all, but a curse.

The presence of choice becomes more apparent the more one chooses with knowledge of the reality that a choice is always in front of them, not an inevitability. When one can no longer escape the determinism of a wrong choice, it is a sign that he has chosen the gift that is not really a gift at all but a curse, and the freedom that is not really freedom at all but a prison, and has become accustomed to the curse and the prison so that choice is no longer apparent—his experience becomes deterministic. Freewill becomes difficult to identify as real at all, because one is thrust into the automation of sin. There were two different gifts, and if man had known how much better the one was than the other, he would have never traded it. Yet God gave His greatest gift to us at the beginning—true freedom under the condition that we acknowledge the truth in that freedom. So true freedom cannot come without a condition. Apart from that condition truth and freedom are divorced. It is the deconstructionists who tell us the condition truly eliminates freedom. By appealing to our fleshly sensualities, often mistaken for our intellectual sensibilities, the lie appears to be truer than the truth as the real paradox of true freedom under the sovereignty of a designated condition becomes a contradiction in our mind's eye. It is the inability to see that we can have everything in one imperfect and corruptible sense only once we have acknowledged that we cannot have everything in another perfect and incorruptible sense which is the first sign of spiritual blindness. It is the only blindness that can be caused by opening our eyes.

Spiritual blindness is why a person cannot create something new but can only refashion the things they already know—and what they refashion always illustrates this spiritual blindness. Can anything fashioned by us truly see, or can we only see through what has been fashioned? People cannot create life, but they can refashion something that imitates a life. People cannot create eyes and ears, but they can create cameras and microphones. People cannot create mind, but they can create databases and algorithms. These images cannot truly see, speak or hear because they don't have life. So the idols are analogous to the secondary human condition which is fallen as a result of the rejection of the primary condition. Can one come up with an example of a creation—something from nothing, living from nonliving—that has been brought forth by mankind? Of course not. Everything has been shaped, wielded, constructed, channeled or molded. This is not to say that man could never have fashioned something from nothing or life from nonlife in his paradise condition. This we cannot know. Although no example of pure creation of mankind can be found, mankind doesn't recognize this fact, but builds what it builds in a fierce rejection of this fact. The *fact* is that the gift of life comes from the creator of life and nowhere else, the *lie* is that one can reject this fact and build new life. The gift from God is as much a gift of life as it is a gift of freedom. The lie is nothing less than a flat out denunciation of our creator, or a soft suggestion which leads to this denunciation. Today we live in a world which denounces the creator, or even anything resembling a mind that is behind the universe—even as all evidence points to exactly that. There is no way to escape the redefinition of the human status as creators in the midst of an existence where humans assume there's no higher mind than their own. Though knowledge screams at us that we lack in our ability to purely understand—let alone to purely create—we pose as the creators nonetheless, as our own gods. Yet the only "logical" thing that this denial of the creator, who is spirit, and denial of the self as created life leads us to is spiritual death. There is no way to escape this spiritual death apart from the Spirit who is life and peace.

The rejection of the true gift is the misappropriation of the gift as something we've earned. This is why the *wages* of sin are death, because we traded the gift for a wage, righteousness for sin, and life for death. The wages become one with our mind because our mind became warped by a sense of divine entitlement. Once we were convinced to see the freedom that we had as something other than a free gift which could not be earned, we were doomed to have the mind of a tradesman who could do nothing more than simply buy and sell. Rest became toil.

True freedom, we thought, had to come at a cost. The cost was the rejection of the condition. The condition was the recognition of the cost. This recognition of the cost could not have been held without the fear of the Lord. The rejection of the condition was also the ultimate rejection of both the understanding of our nature, true freedom, and the One who gave them to us. The free gift became a foreign and hostile concept. This is one reason why it is better to give than to receive, and to give without letting your left hand know what your right is doing. Knowledge of all the benefits of the free gift one is giving makes it no longer a free gift, but a wage with an expectation of recompense.

The same gift can become two quite different things depending on who's looking at it. One is the gift as it undeniably is, the other is a perversion of the gift. The perverse gift is a life that one cannot escape from feeling is earned, and an earned freedom. Earned life is really no life at all. We could not have earned anything before we were anything. Earned freedom is no freedom at all, because we couldn't earn our freedom before we were old enough to become laborers who were free to work for wages. Life and freedom were completely determined for us by another—in this sense deterministic reasoning is correct. For how could one be free to choose freedom, or alive to choose life? There was no life for us before our creation, or freedom for us before our life—therefore life and freedom are always bound up in truth, and that truth is bound up in our creator. We are made in His image, and we're set free by His image. When we abandon His image, death enslaves us.

There is no way to presently deny that this life was a free gift given to us under the condition of our own freedom. Freedom would at once be our undoing and would render a cruel existence without the presence of God—bondage to sin. The free gift would not have been free if it was not given freely. The condition of this gift was not an absence of its freeness. The condition was our recognition of this aspect of the gift. Apart from this recognition there could be neither life nor freedom, for life and freedom would have been earned. Once they became earned we became slaves to toil and birth pains, and the new human gift was corrupted.

One gift is who we are, and the other is who we aren't. When the gift that we were was traded for the gift that we weren't, we became what we weren't and lost sight of who we were. We were suddenly our own creators, thanking ourselves for a gift we couldn't fathom. Seeing the world this way easily answers the difficult philosophical question about why a good and powerful God would allow so much suffering in a fallen world. It is "allowed" because people who reject the very basis of who they are, are bound to suffer deeply in their spirit until they regain consciousness of true life and freedom, which comes by recognition of the condition and the cost of the refusal to recognize it—this spiritual suffering (suffering as a result of sin) is destined to manifest indefinitely in individuals and societies. There can be no existence without suffering in an existence which is subject to decay. There can be no decay without suffering. There can be no loss of life without sadness felt by those who loved that life. There can be no injury without pain. There can be no wrongdoing without a cry for justice.

I stand corrected. There aren't two gifts, but one. The difference is the way in which the gift of God is viewed, whether it is earned or unearned. Since it cannot by nature be earned, and by our nature we all are destined to see it that way, we are unable to see it for what it is. Our blindness must be shown to us. The gift as it is cannot be seen for what it is or even treasured as a gift without the recognition of the condition that it was a gift given unconditionally. It was the reversal of this recognition—the gift becoming unconditional only inasmuch as we carnally reject its spiritual condition—which brought forth the perversion of the human condition in all its tragedy and suffering. For under such conditions no such thing as life, freedom, or gifts could exist as they were originally defined. They could only exist as we gradually redefined them. This was the birth of the new reality.

THE NEXT CHAPTER

The mind of sinful man became death when the gift of life was traded for a lie. The impact of the curse would soon follow the action that led to the curse. The manifestation of suffering, pain and death were soon to follow the first sin, for the first sin opened the door to what mankind could not recognize crouching behind. If mankind was able to recognize the lie as a lie, the lie would have been excluded. The lie was built on the premise of making what was empty seem full and what was full seem empty. True life and freedom were no longer *truly* life and freedom. They were death and bondage. Death and bondage were presented as true life and freedom. The vessel of sin which would lead to death and bondage was seen as the vessel for true life and freedom. As Adam and Eve were introduced to both the presence of a new mystery and the possibility of understanding that mystery, they were at once thrust into doubt of their creator. The fruit was forbidden because it was harmful, but the law of God was transgressed because it was seen to be restrictive. The desire to peek behind the curtain could not be held back for long.

God did not need to have a reason for having one restriction in the garden. He certainly did not need to explain His reasoning to those He created. They were accountable to Him, not the other way around. Satan tricked us all by reversing, among all the other things, this idea of accountability. Many today doubt God's character as much as, if not more than His existence—and for the brief moment an atheist is not discrediting the possibility of a God, the atheist is questioning the motives of the most likely candidate for that God (which begs the question: why do they feel the need to discredit someone who isn't there in the first place if they can disprove Him scientifically?). As logical as it seems to wage war with God on two fronts, it is actually a self-defeating purpose. One cannot harm a fictional character through criticism—and one cannot attack the character of anything whatsoever without a preexisting blueprint for proper character. The atheist critiques the "Old Testament God" for His brutality (wrath, justice and foreknowledge)—but what is their basis for what constitutes brutality after all? This current popular attitude illustrates that true doubt never began with doubting the existence of the creator but the character of the creator. The pinnacle of worldly knowledge and wisdom has only brought us full circle to the garden. Although navigating various doubts and objections seems more insurmountable today than it did in past ages, unbelief was no less present at the beginning.

Mankind fell when it no longer recognized itself as accountable to God, but recognized God as accountable to it. This was the original substance of human folly, which constitutes both a lack of spiritual understanding and a degradation of our moral texture as creatures. These separate losses were bound together from the beginning, for understanding of our place and the goodness of our purpose had to extend from the submission of our will to our good creator who in His understanding structured the place we live in and gave us our purpose in it. This submission of our will is what straightens our path before our creator, making us able to see and understand place and purpose. The promotion of our own will and cultivation of our own vision is what blinds our eyes and paralyzes our will. This *secondary* understanding exists apart from the path of God. It is foolishness to those who belong to God, but unquestionable doctrine to those who are separated from Him.

Humans saw the beginning of their own questionable nature when they first questioned their nature as answerable to the One who provided them with their nature. This first act of rebellion would doubtless be followed by increasing evil, all stemming from the same root of pride. The brother of Able was warned about the condition of pride when he began to entertain it. God warned him, "If you do not do what is right, sin is crouching at your door" (Genesis 4:7). Cain was not told "sin is crouching at your door, therefore do not do what is wrong." There is a clear difference between the state of a person's mind before and after transgression. Even with the first bite, sin was crouching at the door only after the action, for it was after this that the couple's eyes were opened and they realized their nakedness. Being told the lie did not result in the fall from grace, but disobedience that came as a result of believing in the lie. The debate of when and what the sin was exactly continues, but it is answered quite simply in the word "belief." The matter is where we put our faith, for faith is not only thought but deed. Physical action is not always what constitutes *doing* what is right or wrong, but a constant spiritual disposition. When God warned Cain, His warning did not only extend to the actions of his hands but to the complaint of his heart. Falling from grace is not a physical fall, but a spiritual one, and so it is much more real, perpetual, and active than what is purely visible. The physical actions are bubbling manifestations of the spiritual condition, the "tip of the iceberg" so to speak. How can we do what we do not know and how can we know what we do not do?

The fourth chapter in Genesis illustrates the murderous physical result of the fallen spiritual condition. The rejection of true life very quickly showed that a sinful man could not only reject the definition of life on a spiritual level, but could take another life away through physical violence. This is why it simply cannot be a myth that after God's primary law was transgressed, lawlessness entered the world. Our words build our ways and our ways build our worlds. If those words are rooted in the truth of the Father, then our ways will reflect Him, and our world will too. If those words echo the father of lies, then the actions of our hands are soon to follow what echoes in our mind. Considering no man or woman is exempt from the latter condition and only some have been restored to the former, it is logical that our world more tellingly reflects the latter than the former. The question that is often posed to defeat God, "why is there so much suffering in the world," proves the doctrine of original sin, and therefore proves the existence of God as the contrast. A question which is meant to posit doubt as truth, if considered deeply and honestly enough, will advance the truth not only of God but of Christ. For if God is good and He is the creator who is free to create, His creation would not be good if it was not granted the freedom to choose sin or righteousness. This freedom of choice is apparent in our everyday lives. Freedom of choice has not always led to the choicest of freedoms. If we did not have both the freedom of choice and the tendency to sin, we would never have made a mistake in our lives. *Our* freedom of choice specifies *both* a good God *and* the reason "why there is so much suffering in the world." So does the story of Cain and Able.

The pattern of the world system which was the catalyst for pain and suffering cannot reasonably be ignored, nor can the blame of this catalyst be transferred to the one who warned us about it. The repetitive transfer of blame is only sensible to the skeptic because it is taught by the world pattern that bred skepticism.

Cain's sacrifice was not acceptable to God, because it was given out of pride. When the truth was brought to Cain's attention, Cain became envious and angry. The more the lie is threatened, and the more the lie is an important part of our lives, the more threatened our lives feel when confronted by what we can no longer deny. Exposing the persuasiveness of the lie is the first part of the power and authenticity of the gospel. It confronts the world with the truth, the world which is conformed to a set pattern apart from truth and therefore innately unable to recognize it (John 1:10; John 18:37). The language of the gospel shines through the story of pain and suffering, because it was true that God, in His very nature, could not bear to alienate Himself from these things and so He entered into the system of pain and suffering we had created. Yet the truth will not impose its will on another, but will stand at the door and knock. It is the lie that will crouch at the door, awaiting the opportunity to enter our homes in order to kill, steal, and destroy us.

A FLOOD OF INFORMATION

Every day each person is confronted by many things. From the moment we open our eyes to the moment we close them our eyes are filled with the great, the terrible and the ordinary. Even after we close our eyes, dreams continue to pass in our midst. We are unable to control them. In this sense, no one can avoid a flood of information based on their experiences. Even though each person wakes up in submission to reality, held to whatever knowledge comes by experience, each person also seeks knowledge in one way or another. This seeking may be for a knowledge that is healthy and beneficial, or a knowledge that is rooted in wickedness—in self-ascendency and personal glory. Each day the sun is destined to rise and set things either right or wrong. The information that we seek can be an indicator of whether we will amass evil things or good things throughout the day. God commands us not to set any evil things before our eyes. Today, just because we do not spend our time staring at carved images, does not mean we do not have our idols as a culture. In the age of information, one would expect man's desire for a flood of knowledge to have been fulfilled. Yet we are constantly oversaturated with the wrong kinds of knowledge, and always thirsting for more.

At the beginning, humanity fell because of a desire for the wrong kind of knowledge. The temptation of that knowledge said, "Fear not, I am the knowledge you desire." Mankind immediately recognized a desire to have more than it had, even though it had everything. It desired everything in another sense. Yet it was impossible for mankind to recognize the danger of what lay ahead as a result of this choice. Mankind tricked itself into believing that the curse was not there because it couldn't see the curse. What it did see was an appeal to awaken from the dream which had been set before its eyes—Satan succeeded in suggesting that things as they presently were, were not things as they actually are. Satan did not suggest that God the creator wasn't real, but that God's desire for his creation wasn't reality. Man and Woman, confronted by a beast which spoke, were intrigued by its insight. This insight was attainable, declared the beast, and was desirable to achieve the mind of God.

The serpent wasn't lying, in a sense. The easy access to new information would open the eyes of the couple. In fact, they had so much new knowledge that they immediately became afraid, recognizing their own shame and nakedness, and hid in the garden. Paradise was meant to be a place where fear was impossible, yet anywhere that fear is even a possibility a person can find it. God designed us in a way to shield us from entering the territory of shame and nakedness, but mankind's desire for conquest resulted in the inevitable entrance into this territory. All the events that unfolded came as a result of our desire for a knowledge that would raise us up from submission and grant us a new life. This is why every person is destined to drift from God, the spiritual condition of the new man, who really has become the old man, cannot be escaped. It is true that everyone flees from God to this prison of knowledge by suppressing the truth, then becomes isolated within it—both loving and hating it. Loving the pleasure of sin deafens a person. Hatred of the consequences of sin give a person ears to hear the only words that will save them.

The man who loves his sins hates the world in the right sense of the world—this is why he so often asks in his heart why a good and loving God would bring us into such a cruel and intolerable existence. Does indicting existence as cruel and intolerable not display a resentment towards existence, towards the gift of life that comes from God? Meanwhile this man lacks the understanding to recognize that it is his own condition, not God's creative mistake that has made the cruel and intolerable aspects of the world through a resentment of the world and a love for sin. He loves the world in the wrong way too. He suppresses both the truth about God and the truth about himself. So love for the world that stands between him and God is misinterpreted. Those on the side of truth listen to God, and those with a desire for a new kind of knowledge seek the will of the world to corroborate their own will. Because the world is the realm of what can be seen and felt, it is much more manipulative. The world advertises that it is what truly constitutes the whole of reality, not some invisible God. Therefore the visible world affirms and encourages the invisible and faulty spiritual condition as long as the invisible and faulty spiritual condition is prevalent in the visible world. Like the serpent, the systems and patterns of the world it manipulates become craftier as time goes on in how they dupe mankind into digesting the knowledge of good and evil.

The question, "why does God allow suffering?" is a sign of the unbeliever's spiritual peril. It is a sign of the curse. The one who is cursed curses God for existence. This question can only come because of the knowledge of good and evil—the tendency to become judges with evil thoughts, judges who traded God's righteous judgement for our own corruptible set of weights and measures. *We* make the world perverse and then *we* judge its perversity. In our corruption of the world and our corrupt view of the world, we transfer the blame of that corruption to the Father who intended the world to be pure and incorruptible. Anyone who is realistic about this question can see that this is the case. The question of God's character in this day and age is usually prefaced with a question of God's existence. Therefore the person who asks this insults God in two separate ways, he rejects the notion of a God unless that God fits his own idea of a God of cruelty. One can see the original traces of this mindset in the condition of those who first fell, when they saw that God was actually someone other than who He told them He was—one who had taken from them the right to life as they wanted it to be. This inversion was the first step into the abyss of the worldly pattern. From this point on, the worldly pattern was the only acceptable one.

How could God bear to see those that he created and gave the gift of everything (existence), walk along even in the midst of everything while blaming Him for taking everything away from them (suffering)? In other words, if God exists and He is all good and all powerful, why aren't we immediately struck dead when we ask a question that advances Him as evil? That is the more realistic question when God's existence and character are truly considered. The prideful declaration of man's erring judgement over God led to a lot of the world's suffering, suffering that could not be quelled by the evolution of man, by the height of his architecture or bt the increase of his knowledge, but only intensified by them. As long as we carry in our hearts the native tendency to rebel against God, the rebellion of which the question is a universal symptom, the world pattern will become more twisted and unidentifiable as anything meaningful or intended by God.

The question which brought about two floods becomes more realistic than reality only when the world comes to reflect the reality of the wicked human heart more than the reality intended in the good creation of God. The one who is realistic about the question can recognize that the ways of the world are more of an expression of man's faith in the chaos of existence and in his own perceived triumph over that chaos than in God's ability to create, structure, order, and regain victory over a corruptible existence. It is true that what a man puts his faith in will manifest in the world around him. If it is oblivion, so be it. If faith is in his own rule over that oblivion, it can only result in more oblivion, because sin has put him in an oblivious state as the god of oblivion.

Man can gripe to the ground, to the skies, even to the one behind the skies. Little does he know, he is only condemning the curse he brought upon the ground. He is calling forth the wrath of the skies. This is the position of the atheist intellectual, who blames God and not himself for the curse of daily life. The atheist intellectual stands in the rising tide of knowledge of the will of the world and does not recognize he is in danger of drowning in it, but embraces a mood of suicide. Christians see him ask the question and validate him rather than condemn the question. We say, "I see your point," or "great question!" But it's not a great question. It's the first and last great boast of a man to reject his creator before the flood of knowledge covers his head. It is a primary symptom of human folly to deny one's self any part to play in the world's suffering. It was such a flood of wrongheaded intellectualism that caused those who blasphemed God to be stoned for it in the camp of Israel. A man being stoned for blasphemy was simply a clever and fitting rebuke to the man by the ground itself. The stoning of Stephen, on the other hand, showed the way that mankind reacted to God's incarnation that lifted the curse. Humanity had become accustomed to the curse. The curse is so cherished and embraced by humanity that humanity is quick to cast the first stone at the ones in the crowd who know for certain that the curse has been lifted.

In our day and age we are saturated with unlimited information, whether it's good or bad. Our ability to become evil judges in our own hearts has never been more prevalent in the age of information. The tide is rising faster than ever, and worldly wisdom is available in bulk. Yet many today, including secular folk, are able to recognize that this information and knowledge is not rising from the blessing but from the curse. The information sphere of the internet and social media among other things was intended to once again advertise the prominence of the new man, the man who could conquer the ground and skies by shaking his fist at the one who made them. It has also proven to be a great snare to the Christian, who increasingly is being swept up by the tide and unable to recognize that the tide is not a blessing, but a symptom of the curse. It is apparent that, although invisible, this worldly pattern is soon to take us by surprise, even as we laugh and refuse to take it seriously. Of course, I am not solely referring to technology, but to the unlimited reach of man's fist toward the sky, and the increasing efficiency and luster of the tools needed to help get him there. Apparently, mankind is becoming united by one common theme, and is more divided and confused than ever. Just as the rising tide of information reminds us of another biblical tide that could not be forecasted until it suddenly happened, so the manic building of mankind is beginning to look similar to another ancient building which boasted in its ability to rival God.

OBSTRUCTION WORKERS

I have discussed the following concept in depth in my previous two books so I will not talk about it too much here. Yet the example of the Tower of Babel is one of the stories that best prefaces our spiritual condition *as a society*, rather than as individuals. If Adam and Eve reaching for the fruit of the tree to have their eyes opened was the earliest symptom of mankind's spiritual downfall, then this tower certainly is one of the first symptoms of mankind corporately falling into this pattern of the heart as they establish civilization.

The same reaching out of the individual is no less present in today's society when men and women come together to build. Building the Tower of Babel was likely supported as an incredible feat of human achievement and an overall moral good at the time of its construction, but the only glimpse we get of it in scripture shows that it was the broad and detectible manifestation of mankind's cumulative aggression and challenge to God. In the Garden, the couple reached to the highest point they could in a rebellion of spirit; in the plains of Shinar, society likewise reached as high as they could as a community. The result in the first case was a spiritual fall of the inner being. The result in the second case was a communal fall and scattering of the entire world. Although this wasn't the first instance of sin and pride resulting in external chaos and/or death, it was the first recorded instance of the rise and fall of a nation due to pride alone.

The rapid building and coming together of man with an attitude of nationhood and architectural conquest is an expression of a cumulative and ongoing spiritual position of death. Moreover, the degenerating theme of a nation is a symptom of its people's inability to hear or see in the way God originally intended. The first vision of many men together, and their desire to refashion the world to fit their distorted vision, was the first (the most clearly stated and earliest recorded) example of a society literally and figuratively blinded by corrupted ambition. We will call this example *the nation*. The national temperament of Babel was one of pride and immortality, but its real destiny was imminent national demise and humiliation. In this isolated demise was the seed which brought forth all nations to follow. One can clearly see that, in the breaking up of the nation of Babel and the sudden halt to construction of the tower, the individual condition of spiritual blindness—blindness to the way of God—extended to the nation, and then to all nations.

Clearly the national mood is one of immortality, but the reality of the nation is that it faces death as much as if not more than human beings do. Societies and nations are the best human method to either protect and cultivate life or oppress and shatter it—sometimes both at once. A protected person can be internally shattered and an oppressed person can be eternally saved. People who build nations and conquer do it with their own survival and the survival of their nation in mind. But if their attitude shifts from a recognition of their own submission as builders to the will and authority of God to baseless self-worship and high-rising predominance, their demise is more forthcoming than when they were able to recognize how imminent it was. As the pages of history have shown, the Babylonian condition would echo throughout the succeeding epochs, showing that she was the mother of those who were to follow. The sooner the leaders of nations are able to recognize their own limitations with humility the better. It is after we reject those limitations and worship ourselves that our sanity is stripped from us and our empire crumbles. The more we build toward the sky in a spirit of rivalling God, the more we are forced to endlessly labor in futility as our vision, which we think is being widened, becomes progressively restricted.

To analyze the Babylonian equivalent to past and present societies is not a project of creative writing or an invoking of the mythologies of the past to explain the situation of the present. The tower is simply a clear and present picture of the past which warns of what we have presently come from, and the perpetual danger which is always crouching at the door of any nation's future. When the best way to see why the world is the way it is, is by analyzing a compelling spiritual and historical template, we would do well not to scrap this template as pure myth when the phenomenon of Babel re-presents itself in the collapse of many new societies. As far as the nation is concerned, we hold within our hands a recipe for failure. What we do not hold in our hands is a blueprint for a tower which is guaranteed to thrive. That is the point. If we held that blueprint in our hands we would be purely self-reliant. God necessitates the first law of national survival to be deep humility; primarily a humility of the people before God, and secondarily a humble respect for the recipe of failure, an acknowledgement of national mortality. National mortality is the general rule, not the exception. Humble recognition of national death is the first sign of a prolonged national life. National life is the power of people gathered together and in their right minds. National death is the pathetic powerlessness of a people when they are confused, divided, and scattered. The result of a people thus afflicted is to move away and to create new societies which are likewise afflicted. "From there the Lord scattered them over the face of the whole earth" (Genesis 11:9).

I believe the best way to see the present is through the lens of the past. Long lasting nations are predicated on heeding the warnings of past failures. They know what to do and what not to do. It is also good to see the past through the lens of the present. It is arrogant to think we've constantly outgrown our past. We can only realistically chart out the future with this paradox in mind.

The utopian goal which is dreamed up by so many is likely not possible in the way that it is hoped for. The utopian goal is predicated on escaping from the chains of the past. We cannot escape past chains as long as the ground is cursed because of us. Each generation makes clay bricks out of the cursed ground and stacks them endlessly, one upon another. We think we're building out of ingenuity, bringing the curse back up to the sky from which we think it came. The ground is not cursed because of God but because of human sin. He has told us this from the beginning. The warning is the thing we choose not to hear. The vision that seeks to undo the curse purely by the architecture of man restricts the truer vision—the vision of the realism God intended. The tower was not what God intended but what man intended. The mystery of the tower was the threat that God saw within it. Was what He saw an architectural weakness or a fault of another sort? He intervened not because He knew the workers could not manage the task they set out to do, but because He saw that they could do anything they put their mind to.

The sociological condition of Babel is alive and well as people furiously build up modernity. As we "build toward a better future," we should ask ourselves if we are building from a vision of eyes that cannot see danger or eyes that can. Are we listening to the voices and warnings of those who came before us, or do we also have ears that cannot hear? I'd hate to misconstrue Babel to fit our present state. They are different societies under different circumstances. But humanity always seems bound within a prison of its own architecture. God saw on the plains of Shinar that mankind was not constructing the tower in order to break out of this pattern but to fulfill the new law of the new man, corporately. The law of the sinful nature turned out to be the old law of the old man. The desire to escape the patterns of sin and ineffectuality *on our own* destined us to fulfill the imposing, winding, serpentine law of the worldly pattern, which is passing away. The corporate lie teaches us to continue building faulty architecture in two ways: by telling us that we are able to do so without failure—"You will not surely die"; and by telling us that building in this way is sure to bring about a better, more just future—"For God knows that in the day you eat from it, your eyes will be opened and you will be like God, knowing good and evil" (Genesis 3:5). The premises of worldly ambition, ungodly enlightenment, and rebellion against God fueled the construction of the first great tower, which is why its destruction and the exile of its people were soon to follow.

Many societies may acknowledge that they fall into the same configuration. They build from the ground up and the ground is cursed because of them. This recognition is the first sign of a healthy society, a society whose downfall may be slightly less approximate. I don't mean we all ought to live in mud huts and scrap civilization. I think the realization must be more spiritual than that. Collective architecture is bound to represent a spiritual situation. The rejection of God as a society is accompanied by an attitude of soaring pride and then scattered conquest, whether it be by military warfare or prideful ideology. In Babel's case, the ziggurat was formed from a frantic production to enter into the sky, to make it up to heaven on the nation's own steam, and to pave the way for the rest of humanity to walk up this "stairway to heaven" in the same way.

DOOMED TO WONDER

An unprecedented level of confusion followed the construction of the tower in the plains of Shinar. Mankind was cast out of the land they were shaping in order to try and escape the curse and rival God. They did not realize that the curse came in the first place because of man's enmity with God and could only be escaped by a newfound unity with God. The plains of Shinar had an etymology that fulfilled exactly what took place there as recorded in scripture; defeat and exile. The meaning of Shinar is multifaceted, but partly signifies the casting out of a breach. There are two definitions of a breach that fulfill the defeat and exile which occurred to the people at Babel—1) an act of breaking through or failing to observe a law, and 2) a gap in a wall, barrier, or defense, especially one made by an attacking army. Adam and Eve were cast out of the garden for causing a breach in the first sense of the word, the later peoples, whose ambitions were contrary to God's will in the construction of the first great tower, were cast out for the act of trying to create a human-divine breach into heaven. God's language in Genesis 11 signifies a concern that they were going to be able to do what they set out to do if they kept at it.

Even though the building was physical, the motivations were spiritual. Both breaches resulted in a stretching out of the hand towards divine enlightenment, architectural conquest and transcendental power. Both resulted in a fall from grace, in being struck with sudden confusion, and in a wandering heart that set the people on their longsuffering paths outward to the ends of the earth.

In the Garden of Eden, the couple's failure to observe God's law and their desire to burst through to the other side of the law constituted a rebellion of the individual human heart. This rebellion could only result in the casting out of the breach, the punishment of the rebels. Obviously their sin was an action and not only a thought, but it was as much an action of the eye as it was an action of the hand. The vision still causes man to desire to break through God's law and the hand still allows man to follow through with his desire. The desire and the action become one and the same, spiritual and bodily. The action of sin lives within the attitude of sin.

The booming tower casts the shadow of an enflamed and confused heart. It is the result of beguiling sin being the law of the land, reaching skyward from the foundation of the knowledge of good and evil. Babel is much more than a simple allegory (although it certainly tells a powerful story). It is a historical precedent which outlines the doom that awaits the society that furiously builds and omits the awareness of the spiritual breach it is creating. With the Chaldean prototype in mind, we travel into the present.

The new age has caused us to reject the notion of God who's higher and man who's lower. Mankind is *progressively* showing symptoms of the condition of reaching beyond the infinite without any humility, restraint or acknowledgement of spiritual danger. These symptoms emerge daily within distinct and common stages. Individual attitudes and social institutions preserve a defiance against God's enduring quest to "restrict human sovereignty." To deny ourselves any spiritual or material ambitions or pleasures is seen as authoritarian and villainous.

If Adam obeyed God by not eating from the tree of knowledge of good and evil, he could eat from *any other tree* in the garden. God's multifaceted reward for Adam's obedience greatly outweighed the solitary restriction. But there was an inversion of the precept that we had been given everything by God as a reward for one thing—our trust in, love for and obedience to God. The couple's exile from their home showed that their desire for everything (including the one thing they must avoid) resulted in their loss of everything that they knew, the destruction of their home. These ancient patterns are alive and well in every new thing.

The pattern of the breach emerges in a series of different steps: the awareness of a restriction, the contemplation of disobeying the restriction, the action of disobedience, and punishment. This pattern holds true for one person in these ways: we are told that we cannot have something, we see what we want but cannot have without consequence, we take what we want, and the thing ends up resulting in a consequence. The thing and the consequence may vary in weight. The rule of the breach holds true for society in these ways: society recognizes its capacity to fail as a result of its condition, it also recognizes its power and the possibility of transcending this condition, it builds with an attitude of conquest and pride, and then it falls into madness and destruction. The punishment seems to always take the form of environmental calamity, genocide and warfare, or widespread poverty.

In society today, a person is assaulted on three fronts with the attitude of transgression. Spiritually, the condition of the new age preaches our own inherent divinity and affirms our own likeness of the gods. Intellectually, the dogma of naturalistic materialism brainwashes us into thinking that we are nothing more than matter in motion—there is no spiritual component at all to the patterns that pervade creation and there is no God. Society comes together out of this binary outlook to build preschools and space programs. We are blindest to the spiritual component of rebellion against God which would remind us of the cosmically enduring pattern of sin and evil and which allows nothing new to come underneath the sun. As long as we remain spiritually stubborn, spiritual understanding remains inaccessible. This barring from the garden of truth comes as a result of ungodly ambition and the constant fulfilment of the flesh.

No matter how spectacular the things we build as societies appear at the time of their construction, when they emerge from the demise of the spirit and from the curse of the ground, they are structurally unsound. As we see the breakneck construction today, we would be foolish not to recognize the signs that production could cease at any moment. These signs have been clearly and recently shown in the harmful results of certain leaders' and people's conceited visions, leaders and people who desired to bring about the most evolved forms of humanity, but left humanity deformed by social engineering experiments, demolished cities, scorched earth and torturous prison camps. The quest for knowledge and superior architecture has manifested in many forms of modern technology and new theories—the age of information, social media and the space race—but has led to many dangers including totalitarianism, war, human isolation, addiction and despair.

The age of information is a fascinating case study of how humanity operates with easy access to all the knowledge we could possibly fathom. Some may argue that easy access to this information has largely dulled the human capacity for authentic reason. People are no longer forced to work hard to come to conclusions or to weigh out the correctness and honesty of information. The tools they use are also designed to maintain a level of control over the way they spend their time and money and over their general mindset. Technology such as computers, the internet, search engines, and social media were all designed to be used as tools that enhance the human experience. They were likely not designed with a grand conspiracy of control in mind. However, as the capacity of the technology increases in its ability to read and manipulate us by reforming the information we receive, the capacity for people to recognize one another's genuine perspectives diminishes. This is likely the closest sign to a modern universal confusion of language. It came from the intent to connect us all under a common goal or interest. The tools for communication on a global scale have reached their pinnacle while the ability for people to listen to and understand one another is at an all-time low. If there's one thing the second technological revolution is teaching us, it's that humanity doesn't know how to handle omniscience.

Humanity doesn't want to stop at omniscience either, for how could it be as God without omnipotence too? As a society and a "species," we have an unshakeable preoccupation with the stars—not to mention a desire to continue to break through new levels of space travel. Ever since the fifties, sci-fi shows like Star Wars and Star Trek have captivated people. Some philanthropists and intellectuals are now focusing their resources on outsourcing humanity's future to the far reaches of space. The space race can be recognized as something more than humanity's desire to push its limitations in a healthy, spiritually neutral way. The space race is nothing more than an outworking of mankind's delusion that we can break through reality itself and finally shake hands with our own transcendence by conquering the stars. There is likely no greater modern parallel to the great futile tower which sought to breach the heavens, and the Babylonians also had a significant preoccupation with cosmology. I understand that the space race is an extremely touchy subject for many people. Many put so much faith in space agencies that any critique of their motives causes controversy. But as Christians, maybe we ought to be aware of these parallels and to critique ourselves when we put too much faith in the systems of man.

I titled this chapter with a play on words in mind. A person's quest to obtain total knowledge and mastery over everything may be more telling of their powerlessness than their power. When someone grasps for everything it shows that he doesn't actually have anything. The world around us is quite simply an affirmation of the doctrine of Original Sin, especially the shinier and more technologically advanced it becomes. This may be telling not only of our desire to breach the doors of heaven with battering rams rather than to enter by God's invitation, but to create a new heaven right here on earth with prior knowledge that the doors cannot be breached.

KNOWLEDGE OR CONFUSION?

Around the world there is a tightening stranglehold on the church. Dozens of countries persecute Christians outright, either systemically or communally. And in the Western world, many Christians are sensing some type of persecution looming. It's hard to claim that we are being persecuted in the same way that someone in India, Nigeria, or China can say with confidence that they are being harmed for representing Christ. What happens to Christians in places like the US, Canada, and the UK is much more psychological. It's undeniable that many Christians in these countries face mocking, slander, hatred, job loss, and other consequences for standing boldly for the Gospel. Much of this persecution grows out of an intellectual soil that has been tilled for decades, even centuries.

The postmodern pastiche of ideals predicts that there are an infinite amount of interpretations for any given event or theme. There is an air of correctness in this assumption. It also dangerously assumes that no interpretation can reasonably be placed higher or lower in its degree of truthfulness. This notion merges with pluralism and relativism. Pluralism is the fundamental acceptance of all belief systems, and relativism is the notion that anyone's standard of good or evil is completely subjective, diluting any distinction between the two. These three ideals—postmodernism, pluralism, and relativism—appear to be different branches of the same root system. Also connected to this system are Marxism, Secularism, and Privatization. All of these elements are deeply connected to historical intellectual benchmarks and all contribute to the rise of persecution. This begs the question, as postmodernism would assume that there can be no reasonable joining between such religious belief systems, does the identifiable linking between these themes that have outlasted any individual, nation or generation indicate a non-human source for these belief systems?

Marxism is fundamentally connected to postmodernism as both notions emerge from an intellectual critique of reality as it stands—all institutions, beliefs, and power structures must be deconstructed to bring about a more fair form of rule (Marxism) or thought (Postmodernism). Marxism arguably led to the highest level of persecution of the church in history by multiple communist regimes.

Marx himself deeply hated Christians and Jews. Even the holocaust which killed about 6,000,000 Jews and about 1,000,000 nonconformist Christians was rooted in a socialistic, pantheistic, secularistic sentiment.

A more recent, westernized, secular thought exploration has emerged among the modern moment. Thought leaders like Yuval Noah Harari are paving the way for a new system of thought that ambitiously hopes to perfect all the imperfect past systems like Communism and other forms of totalitarianism. This perfection hopes to come from the merging of secularism with technology and globalism. Dr. Harari lays out the foundation for why secularism is the best form of thought and rule for the modern epoch, but behind his words lie a deeply mendacious, anti-Christian sentiment, which if fulfilled would leave the church silenced, crippled, persecuted, and marginalized. His words allow the church freedom inasmuch as it never contradicts or questions the higher secularized belief system.

Privatization is a natural outcome of all the prior brainwashing up to this point. Privatization is the idea that Christians should not, and in some cases cannot legally proclaim their faith publicly. Many countries have incorporated this attack on Christian freedom into the law of the land. Many people who are deeply pantheistic, secular, or Marxist have it in their heads that Christians may not ever speak about Jesus to them. They see this as hate speech. Meanwhile, they are permitted to preach their antireligious religion far and wide, and escape any accountability whenever its ideas prove to be destructive in the real world.

Even though western countries like America do not face persecution like other countries where Christians are being murdered or imprisoned for their faith, the psychological groundwork for persecution is being laid in the western world in a way that likely dwarfs these other countries. Such a network of ideologies may well make repentance and spiritual understanding much more difficult than in a country where people hate Christians but don't really know why. It also may well be instilling a deeply demonic and genocidal sentiment that sees humanity itself as a growing cancer that needs to be "treated."

MOUTHS, BUT CAN'T SPEAK

The inability to communicate can be a sign of our spiritual condition, which arises from deception. In the beginning of scripture, the inability to communicate, as well as the misinterpretation of the message to be received were largely a cause and effect of mankind's fall from grace. The serpent's deception was not as much an outright lie as it was a perversion of the truth. The deception in his persuasion of Eve was rooted in knowledge of what was already true (law; reality) and the means of manipulating that truth to fit his own purpose (desire; rebellion). Deception sometimes reflects the desire to manipulate what is true for one's own end, rather than to circumnavigate truth entirely. The longsuffering power and presence of sin was born out of deception, and therefore ongoing deception is what is most responsible for the present weakness of human nature.

We have all felt the effects of lies, though often we do not realize that it is truly a lie which has so affected us. Lies are crafted with the intent to hide their own nature from their victims. This is why there is always an invisible element to the corruption within the world pattern, and why it is so often difficult to perceive when we stand apart from the truth, for the truth recognizes the lie for what it is. If the world pattern was transparent about its own corruption, people would recognize its failures and turn from it. However, the world pattern is precise in its ability to camouflage because of its complexity and diversity of ways, which advertise themselves as alternative yet equal paths—complexity and diversity validate the confusion intended by the deceptive world pattern. This thought is predicated on replacing faith in God with an alternative winding and amorphous belief system, whether it be the worship of false Gods (materialism, pantheism, and polytheism) or self-worship (intellectualism and new age).

The world pattern emerges from the depravity of the human spirit as a result of following the lie. So the pattern lies within our history, politics, culture and institutions. The depravity of the human spirit continually emerges from and contributes to the consistency of the world pattern and the reaffirmation of the lie within it. Both of these were and are reliant on an outside spiritual source who has existed throughout the world's lifespan for their survival. This is why Christians must consistently be weary of the world, the flesh, *and the devil*. The world is the impact of society on us as a result of external deceptive and selfish behavior. The flesh is our own internal selfish ends which reproduce this behavior in the world around us. And both of these are dependent on and reinforced by an invisible influencer who exists outside our material sphere for the spiritual consistency and seemingly eternal structure of sin to continue within the world pattern and the pattern of the flesh. Most who have given it some thought, have come to realize that this consistency and structure is remarkably present alongside the history of the world pattern, outlasting any particular individual, nation, government or ideology. Yet in the diversity of the world pattern, the confusion that arises between people and within their conscience gives way to an attitude of chaos and randomness. This stems from the knowledge of good and evil, and therefore the weeds that choke the fruit of true liberty disguise themselves as being the very fruit they choke. Freedom in the way God intended it is taught to the generations that do not know Him as slavery.

In reality, the pattern is quite simple. Its simplicity can be seen in the pages of human history and in the modern repetition of evil and corrupt human behavior which reproduces the stains on those pages. The teacher of Ecclesiastes, in God's Wisdom, was able to recognize two things about everything within the world pattern; there is nothing new that happens under the sun, and all that takes place in the world pattern is meaningless. There is an intergenerational monotony and senselessness that humanity cannot deny. This condition maintains the spiritual muteness of humanity's voice and makes the voices of dumb idols the only voices we are able to hear under our condition *unless we come to recognize the vanity of that condition.*

There is no message to be communicated that has not been communicated already and the one that is consistently being communicated does not matter at all, no matter how much it promises great worldly gain. Although this recognition is the most depressing reality imaginable, it is also the most liberating—for in communicating this message of mundaneness and meaninglessness, the teacher was actually able to communicate a new message to the people, one which broke away from the forms of similitude and insignificance. This is why he was considered exceedingly wise.

The repetitive configurations of the world system enslaved us and tricked us into believing that they were all there is, but the teacher in Ecclesiastes was able to recognize that the patterns were only the symptom, never the cure for the human condition. His diagnosis of the condition that we are all old men and women who are enslaved within an ancient worldly system, was also hinting at a prescription for a way to escape this condition.

The first step on the course to freedom is the recognition of our slavery. The recognition of the world pattern accompanies the realization that we are *hopelessly* entangled within it. In order to escape from our sins we must realize that we can never escape from sin by our own power. The realization of our helplessness is therefore the second most effective message that can be communicated. The condition of helplessness endangers people to hopelessness without the outside source who is the antidote to the worldly influencer. So hopelessness, meaninglessness, futility and vanity are passing away, which means they are still alive. There is no other creed that illustrates this concept more fittingly than the Gospel. The Christian recognizes that the glory of his redemption through Christ was only made possible by recognizing the inescapability of his spiritual situation. The abounding complexity of the world pattern is exactly what enslaves it to redundant simplicity as it dies, whereas the simplicity of the gospel frees the child to discover its complexity as he grows.

Until we confess the name of the one who spoke us into being, we all are silent, no matter how loud we cry at the heavens. Our words are jumbled and meaningless as long as they refuse to acknowledge the meaning of the Word who was there at the beginning, who designed meaning. Rebellion against God made so much of human history bland, bitter, confused, nihilistic and episodic. As long as there is a denial of the beginning, the end and the author who stands outside both, there can be no structure to the story. Instead, the story becomes a painful and confusing montage of generations who were all unable to interpret the disjointed pages in which they were written, even as they continued writing those pages. This pride led to a new type of totalitarian greatness in the world's story that was also a smallness in the eyes of God.

In order to explain the way to others, we must know the way ourselves. The way must always lead from one place to another if it is to be a *way out*. In order to have mouths that are able to speak the truth we must be united to the Word who embodies truth. In order to heal and bring life, we must know where life comes from. As long as the way is bleakly relative and we can make up any old way, there is no point in discussing which way is which. Who's to tell me that I must go their way and not my own in a land of equal paths? As long as the truth is predicated on ideas from the self or symbols interpreted in the world pattern, it is pointless to discuss it as a truth that stands outside at all. There is no satisfactory system set in place to evaluate it as truth or a lie other than the deceptive human will and the corrupted human law. As long as we deny the true definition of life, our own lives and the lives of others will become more and more meaningless (this meaninglessness isn't necessarily linked to depression or negative life circumstances; it often looks like happiness, riches, fame, and glory). The denial of God's true identity and the character of His Son result in the unrecognized growth of evil as long as we hold on to our inaccurate weights and measures. According to Christ, apart from belief in His identity, we are doomed to perish in our sins.

The above explanation shows a great mystery. Our words are despairingly lost until they are found by the Word. This is the only way to escape the lie that ensnares every life. While the symbols and stories of scripture hold the key to unlocking the pages of human history, the depth of human psychology, and the remedy for human failure, Christ Himself holds the key to interpreting those symbols and stories as the Word who stands at both the beginning and the end. He also entered right into the middle, splitting time itself in half. Without Christ our language would become progressively chaotic and confused as we grew within and built upon the faulty foundation of the knowledge of good and evil.

There is no reason to continue building on a faulty foundation once we are made aware that it is faulty. There is no reason to eat from an alluring tree if we are told that we must not or we'll die. Continuing within the way of the world is the recurrent birth of ungodly language, a language which cannot be understood or spoken apart from the communication of spiritual deception that encourages continued building upon the faulty foundation. As challenging as it may be to hear this, it is often simple truth that will aptly speak to our past and present predicament.

Desire for total control over our lives has left us with the mentality that we can be our own gods. The refusal to submit our own will before the one true God has resulted in an age old spiritual death and the inability to be what we actually are. Instead we are quasi-divine organisms, the most evolved bacterium, caught up in a struggle to survive as the fittest and then to become omnipotent and omniscient, constantly speaking words set on fire by the underworld in order to assert our own superiority over others and to be the greatest. But we do not always obey this law of lawlessness, the law of a lawless world, because we cannot escape God's imaging in us. At times we look at others with love and compassion. We feel deep within us joy, hope, peace, and selflessness nagging in contrast to the lawless law, for God has set eternity in our hearts. We may speak for the benefit of others at the expense of ourselves, disobeying the survival of the fittest model. No matter how we deny the meaning of the scriptures and the existence and character of God the creator, we are always case bound to operate under some conditions of the reality that God orchestrated or initially intended, even if those conditions contradict the naturalistic law that one professes to follow, unnatural as it may be.

The louder we speak, and the bigger words we use do not necessarily signify higher standards of truthfulness. After all, all things were created by, for, and through *one* Word, and this Word became flesh to save our flesh. He appeared foolish to shame the wisdom of this world. He became weak to shame the strong. He submitted to the singularity of death to effectuate the big bang of the resurrection. The greatest things may be spoken to us in the quietest of times. The still, small voice always-already holds creation in His hand. One day, God the Father will peel back the sky like a scroll in His final revelation, a scroll which has testified to Christ since its first word, even before He made Himself known.

EYES, BUT CAN'T SEE

There are *two ways* to see the world, two visions that conflict with one another at every turn. All things beheld by the eyes can be beheld either as a sign or a symptom. When God dried up the land and sent Noah and his sons out from the ark, God showed Noah a sign. The sign would remind the nations and generations of God's power to destroy as well as His promise not to. Rainbows were the sign within the heavens of God's covenant with mankind. Mankind apart from God cannot understand the meaning of rainbows even as it scrutinizes them down to the last water molecule. Those who see rainbows in this scientific way would criticize the man who sees rainbows in the mythological context of Genesis as ignorant. We are lost in a world of myths and fairytales. Yet we see those who see the rainbow as a random, meaningless arrangement of light and water molecules as living in a world of myth, an even more dangerous myth.

Some see through eyes that they have not been given, eyes they have given to themselves. Their eyes, as much they were created, have been taken away and replaced by uncreated eyes. These are eyes that see God either nowhere or in all things, not all things as being made through God. These eyeless eyes form the eyes of blind idols. Idolatry is partially the tendency to worship the gift and not the giver of the gift. Worshipping the gift grants the gift its own craftsmanship, even after we crafted it. This worship of a neutral (material) gift robs it of its neutrality and corrupts it. When we worship the things our hands have made, we rob God of His authorship of us. We even rob ourselves of our own authorship of what we make from the things of the earth. We forget ourselves as creatures, we abandon our humility, and we lose out on pure creativity in the process. A symptom of self-worship, worship of creation, and worship of the things our hands have made is a base mind, a mind that is focused solely on the things of this world and the things that we've made out of this world. It is hard to turn from this vision. It takes nothing less than the renewal of our minds.

The eyes that have seen the world in this corrupted way are also the eyes that have made the world what it is. It is this vision that has built up and torn down each civilization, showing the height of man's reach, and the inescapability of his fallen nature. Humanity has always reached toward immortality and utopia, but its hand has always returned to working the ground by the sweat of his brow, oppressing others for one's own benefit, and breathing one's last. The lust for the knowledge of the gods has not added length to our lives, but has reduced us to all the evils that plagued the human experience so far. In our quest for divinity, we fell into our animal nature, even our more diabolical forms. This is what we evolved *into*, not from. We have found our love for nature, and grown in animosity towards our fellow men. The world that was built by the blind ambition of pride has left us bereft of sense, terrified by our vulnerabilities and overwhelmed by our self-perception as gods. This leads many to an attitude of suicide, which is at once an act of fear and cosmic judgement. We remove ourselves from the world because we've judged the world as falling short of our own corrupt law. This belief system removes God from his place and puts ourselves into it. On earth we claim innocence, even sovereignty, but we always stand guilty of a sinful mind which leads to death—the utmost act of pride and also the end result of pride.

The dangers of the vision of pride manifest all around us, but are usually impossible to see within ourselves. We go through life certain about the imperfections of the world and the people around us while remaining unconvinced about our own imperfection. Disregarding our folly is being wise in our own eyes. As King Solomon said, "There is more hope for a fool" than someone like that (Proverbs 29:20). We are all like that at one point or another. At least one who lacks knowledge of the world is not always bent on self-promotion at the expense of others. It is the one who is educated into his worldly sensibilities who seeks to be the fittest and climb the social ladder, no matter who he has to kick off of it on the way up. The problem with evil, its enigma as it is related to human pride is evil's invisibility within the self and its identifiability among others. We know when we are wronged but we so often don't know when we wrong others. This is the source of hypocrisy among other things, which is alien to the one who lives fully in truth. Christ saw pride, self-righteousness, and hypocrisy as three unnatural dangers of sin. They are sin's most visible forms in God's eyes and the most invisible in ours (Matthew 7:5). Hitler's unbelief, pride and hypocrisy were alive long before he brought about the final solution. The recognition of the human condition in others is a given no matter the paradigm, but the recognition of the human condition in the self is truly remarkable. Recognizing the symptoms of an illness is the first step towards healing. But "toughing it out" can be deadly.

To acknowledge that God exists and is higher than you is a prerequisite for humility. It takes awe and inspiration to pray and inquire of God. It takes God to make a man, not the other way around. The reversal of this precept is the beginning of idolatry in many expressions, when we make our own gods to worship. Also, self-worship begins with the inability to see what is higher outside oneself alongside what is lower within oneself, to see our own spiritual incapacity. There is no escaping this prison in our own strength. God has designated the inevitability of the curse for His own purpose, to trick the curse. Fear can lead to a search for courage. Pride can lead to a search for humility. Hatred can lead to a search for love. Lies can lead to a search for truth. A life sentence grants dreams of escape. The problem is that these things can also become so familiar that a person may not want to leave the border walls of unbelief. A departure from the prison shows that a rebuke of the prison's parameters was necessary, that the home we've built for ourselves cannot stand forever. It can feel like death to be exiled from what we know. But just as a seed is dropped into the ground, and must break its shell before growing into something beautiful, so a man must die to himself if he is to live to God and others. The truth is that death has already been crucified on our behalf, the only thing that must die now is the part of us that is dead to God, and that is heading toward the slaughter anyway.

To turn back from a path that leads nowhere is the most progressive thing a person can do. The farther we travel on a path to nowhere, the more we believe the path will lead us somewhere. The more we are convinced of this, the more influential we become in leading others in the same way. The narrow path is much more than the alternative to this, it is the only way around broad and destructive faith. It is narrow precisely because it is the path less traveled. It is less traveled because it is less visible to the world.

I am grateful for the many material treasures of civilization—running water, electricity, automobiles, heated homes, the stock market, thanksgiving dinner, laptops and smartphones. But I am also convinced that each civilization emerges from an inescapably broad and popular vision, the vision of mankind's transcendence by its own strength, no matter how new the age appears. It is this self-perceived transcendence of any given age that grants the illusion of newness to its people. Scripture tells a very different story. One thing it shows is that civilizations rise and fall by God's permission. A civilization's rejection of God seems to be the signature of its own death warrant. The rise and fall of a nation take place first in the hearts of men.

MOTION

Every person sets out on a quest to get from one place to another. This quest can be as small as getting from our bed to our bathroom sink to brush our teeth first thing in the morning, or as great as lifting ourselves out of lasting poverty and into luxury. The way we "go through the motions" each day is a major indicator of what kind of eyes and ears we have, and what kind of people we are. Just as there are two kinds of hearing and two kinds of vision, there are two kinds of motion. The world would argue with me about this, claiming that there are countless ways to move about in it today. After all, people are *visibly* scrambling about in many different directions. In the eyes of the world, seeing all ways of life as a result of only two types of movement is a narrow view. To the Christian it is glaringly true. It is the only thing that is true about movement, and is the most powerful way to interpret the times.

The difference in identifying the Christian view of movement and the world's view is whether we see them as means or ends. Those who trust in themselves see everything as a means to their own end, falling into a symptom of the curse which is both to manipulate and to be manipulated by their brethren. Those with the vision of heaven try their hardest to recognize that without God's help they are doomed to manipulate and be manipulated as well. As soon as they submit their will to his, however, they are free to see the end already, and do not desire to treat encounters as a means to an end, for they only find meaning in God's end and not their own—they are the means to God's end, God's plan is the end to their means. They have already found the end, even from the beginning. It would therefore be meaningless to try and rewrite the end for personal gain. The end becomes our neighbor, not ourselves. The means are the goods we have to attain that end, but this precept is so often reversed when all we have is used only to fulfill the desires of our flesh.

Christ saw so much human movement for what it really was. He and the prophets before Him were able to speak to the heart of mankind and its culture powerfully for this reason. He troubled humanity's view of what's truly important to run after and what's not. He recognized those who were invisible to the world and challenged those who climbed endlessly upward to make themselves the most visible. He saw eating and drinking as a symbols for the deepest truths in the universe. He saw open acts of unrestrained power, toil, oppression and selfish wisdom as futile, even deadly. In other words, He called the least great and the greatest least.

The world pattern is, has always been, and will always be an inversion of what God has seen as truly important. We so often chase after money, power, recognition and sex as ends within themselves, seeing everything *and everyone* along the way as a means to those ends. These are systems which we've convinced ourselves are living, breathing and eternal. We can only use these systems as an extension of one of the two kinds of movement, which moves out from one of the two kinds of words, which speak out from one of the two kinds of knowledge. The first movement arises from a recognition of the system itself as the goal. The second movement already knows that system's only benefit is as a tool to glorify God and to lift others up. Everyone finds their vitality in one type of movement or the other. Whether a person lives as a victim of the curse or as a beneficiary of the blessing depends on what they work towards to bring them life.

In reference to the fall as the template, we can see that the former view of vitality was the temptation of the fruit, its luster and sensual wisdom. It was to become the truly life-giving thing, but it became the thing that took true life away. In a similar way, all the goals and movements of the pattern of the world which appear to be grand gestures to the human eye (landing on the moon, inventing the IPhone 13, free scaling a massive cliff, amassing billions of dollars, amalgamating many world governments into one global entity) may be pathetic in the eyes of God. To worship the things of this world is what it means to have our understanding darkened and to be futile in our thoughts. The things we do are so often a continuation of the rejection of God and His ways, and then a rejection of the truest aspect of our own nature. Our being is a product of God's design, not of our own will. The smallest movements in recognition of God's total authority bring us meaning, while the largest movements in response to our own ambitions rob us of meaning and reform the world around us into one giant carved image.

God's immutable ability to create resulted in His creation, which is the closest thing we can *see* to infinity. But this finite infinity emerged from God's infinite creative goodness. Each person knows this in their heart of hearts—that what they perceive to be everything always is actually neither eternal nor infinite at all, no matter how many quarks, gluons, eons and branch-universes are attached to this eternal infinity. Anyone who denies creation its authorship has suppressed the truly infinite because of the truly infinite's inconvenience to us. They have ambitiously re-created the heavens and the earth and all that is in them, stretching out their hands in worship to a false and futile infinity. In mankind's desire to free itself from its own nature as a creature, it has placed itself in bondage to a cruel master as a product of a lifeless, robotic system. This is the result of worshipping created things, which are defined as everything we are able to see and feel in this world. Paul warns against doing anything from a mindset of faithlessness, which happens to be everything we do in our sinful nature—whether it is reading the newspaper that tells of the world pattern or driving to work to participate in it. It is not the motion and whether we think it to be mundane or futile, good or evil, but the attitude that fuels the motion that makes it either meaningful or meaningless. Motion is meaningful only if there is someone who truly knows the way to life who is behind its attitude. It is meaningless if there is nothing but a lifeless system that powers it.

It is a truly ordinary task to tell the world that the things we touch and see and listen to are all connected, but it is only an existence with meaning that can draw any two distinct connections at all. Removing that meaning results in the impossibility of life itself, for life is meaningful. It is existence apart from meaning which results in the curse—the inability to see things for what they really are, to hear and to understand, and to act effectively as we fear God. No matter where a civilization is—whether in its constructive, stationary, or destructive phase, and whether in famine or prosperity—civilization operates at some level under the guise of a lifeless, winding, predatory, and serpentine system. The ability to see the meaninglessness in worldly things (not necessarily to be confused with material possessions and human achievements, but material possessions and human achievements can certainly be a part of this system) is the first step toward deriving an inheritance of meaning. The inability to see this is a sign of spiritual peril.

FROM THE HEIGHT OF THE HEAVENS TO THE DEPTHS OF THE SEAS

There is no way to wrap our minds around the relative scale and weight of everything, let alone to see and to understand all of it. Yet this is what mankind has done, or claimed to have done. Humanity claims total sight and total mastery over knowledge, and postulates the reality of existence itself as ready to be interpreted by those with total sight and mastery. The distinction between the way in which the faithful view creation and naturalists view nature is in the perceived power of the human race, where that power comes from, and what that power is to be used for. The overview of man's vision, rather his two types of vision, gives clear insight to the destructive nature of human pride and the restorative nature of humility.

For those who believe in everything they touch, taste, feel, and see to be components of a creation with intelligence behind it, everything becomes just another thing in a sense—because it cannot by its *nature* be everything. If it were by its nature everything, it would have had to have been everything, even before it was anything. (This is a dilemma of pantheism.) Therefore everything and all the aspects therein cannot by their nature contain objects or ideas which are worthy of our worship, even taken altogether as the largest universe we can imagine. Whatever is the object of worship must take precedent over everything we are able to interpret or focus on, so it becomes the lens through which we see and interpret everything. The object itself eludes interpretation, which is why it ends up being worshipped, loved with all one's heart, soul, strength and mind. Creation itself is impossible to interpret, which is why it's so often worshipped. The same goes for angels and demons, a beautiful piece of art, exceeding wealth, a beautiful woman, or a great career. As creator, though, God must at once be higher than the heavens and lower than the depths, over all, through all, and in all His people, able to intervene in any aspect of His creation, but not synonymous with His creation. He must also remain unseen in order for there to be a distinction of understanding that emerges from the freedom of choice He's given us.

Nature in the godless sense does not require anyone preceding, outliving or transcending itself to have been established or recognized as someone worthy of reverence, or any attention at all for that matter. Nature is self-created, self-contained, self-described, self-inhabited, and self-oriented. God becomes the other, an alien threat to the survival of this selfish worldview. In order for the eyes of material to be opened, the eyes of the spiritual had to have been closed. Believe it or not, everything in history is contingent on this principle of the two distinctive understandings of the true nature of everything in history. War, peace, famine, thriving civilizations, world decay and injustice have all surrounded people who are competing for the prevalence of their worldview in a state of god-like-ness. Since the dawn of man, manmade architecture—whether in structure or language—has evolved throughout the various challenges made by man to his architect. Therein lies the blindingly hidden nature of idolatry, and why its deceptiveness is so apparent, yet also so vague and difficult to define. The interpretation that gives an idol any power or form requires the contrasting actuality of Yahweh from which true power and form come, as well as the understanding that all forms of sin and evil emerge from rebellion against Him.

If we do not acknowledge the One who made heaven and earth and all that resides therein, we are doomed to spiritual blindness as we lie in wait for the opportunity of worldly advancement. Naturalists reproach the faithful for their proclaimed dominion of man over the beasts of the field and the birds of the air, but they themselves claim intellectual dominion over the earth and sky and everything in them—including the faithful. They hold in their hand the "theory of everything" to once and for all take the place of God and the promise to usher in a utopian kingdom of man to take the place of the Kingdom of God. The dominion of man did not emerge because man proclaimed dominion for himself, but because the One who created man and all else proclaimed an incorruptible dominion for him, a dominion of purity and peace. When our view of His dominion over us was corrupted, our dominion over nature was also corrupted. We selfishly sought power as gods, which is why the creation cries out for the true sons of God to be revealed. This revelation from God undoes the ongoing corruption and perversion of the curse.

The wisdom of the world declares the acknowledgment of this revelation to be a Christian pride that is far too terrible to allow continued life, while the wisdom of heaven considers the revelation of how much a man really means to his creator and his inhabited world as the utmost symbol of humility—this humility is the establishment of right rule, something humanity has only grasped at sincc the fall. Godly humility always resists bowing to unworthy and worldly things, so it seems like the opposite of humility to those who will bow. The truly prideful will bow to anything else before they bow to God. The confusion occurs within the differing definitions of dominion. The faithful recognize true dominion only after they recognize the failure that has come from a perverted will to dominate. The unfaithful claim an unquestioned dominion and reject any notions of spiritual or intellectual fallibility under the pretense of having eyes that are wide open.

The dominion of man can only succeed beneath a humility before God. Those who reject the notion of man's authority over nature are the ones who end up dominating nature unfairly because of the perverse way in which they view the nature of things, as if everything in nature rules over us. If nature has not come from the mind of God, then it must be reborn, reformed, and remade from the mind of man. It must be ransacked, mined, industrialized, and advertised. Mankind, in its selfish nature, will continue to manipulate nature to fit the vision of nature's more natural form—blind, deaf and dumb idols. Blame is placed on those who have faith in what the Word says about man's relationship with nature and our God given dominion. Thus we have today a rotting world and the faithful who are seen by the world to be the decomposers of that world, rather than its preservatives. The faithful see the world for what it is. It is not our God.

There is truth in the ancient stories of the wrath of the gods upon the children of men, of the massive deluge which made all but a few extinct, and of the subjection of the world to decay as a result of the eyes of humanity being opened in one way, and shut in another. This decay was always spiritual before it was corporeal. It still begins with the act of turning defiantly away from God and toward the object of our desire.

The height of the heavens and the depth of the seas are not always large enough containers to hold the height of pride and the depth of depravity. This is why we can never dig deep enough, or build high enough. We do such things to fill an emptiness. This emptiness was a part of our initial design. It was put in place to point us to God, and to reach toward him with open hands rather than closed fists. Both the naturalist and the creationist are reaching toward something more, but the manner in which they reach is widely different. One reaches toward the stars with an intent to one day master them, the other reaches toward the stars with the intention to one day meet the master of them.

I must admit, even as a self-proclaimed faithful servant, how quickly my attitude can shift, and how easily susceptible I am to the attitude of pride. This is in no way intended to be a description of the perfection of the faithful, but a description of why the faithful are able to recognize their imperfection as well as their importance in the scope of creation. When we doubt our imperfection as a result of doubting the perfection of our creator, we imprison ourselves within the same totalitarian nature of genocidal tyrants and divine usurpers.

LIFE AND DEATH CIRCUMSTANCE

One of the signs of the struggle of the modern church is its inability to see everyday perils. An ancient prayer of salvation made danger yesterday's news. The joy of the church experience in its recreation and entertainment faculties have promised us a piece of the world if we will simply sit still for a moment and listen to the heavenly message. The message has to have danger attached to it in order for there to be a sense of adventure, otherwise there is simply the false promise of unfathomable power with no strings attached. Christ never falsely advertised Himself and neither is it our job to falsely advertise the gospel but to preach it, or else we rob the Holy Spirit of His power to convict. It is a dangerous game that the church plays at times, especially if we are trying to transform ourselves into a more palatable form of the church—a church that tastes a little less salty than old Christianity.

Instead of this, the church ought to remind the world that God exists and who He is—padded pews and high production value is nonessential. In fact, catering to comfort may send a separate message even if the new church's intention is true. The more the church blends with my home life, the more likely it is that my home life will stay the same after church. I am not rejecting the comforts of church, and the new church experience as contrary to our goals, but acknowledging that in the midst of the truth, the power of these things becomes secondary and empty. It is precisely Christ's command that we forsake our old lives when we turn to follow Him.

The plain truth is that everyone who walks through the church doors are coming to hear precisely what is contrary to what the world says, not a Christianized version of it. Truth can be the deepest desire of the spirit and the single greatest fear of the flesh. The flesh desires anything but the true message, and so many come for an experience of carnal solidarity. Everyone, Christian or not, is in the midst of that battle and therefore faces danger. The words they hear will either appeal to their flesh or their spirit, but never both.

Romans 8 tells how creation awaits in eager expectation for the sons of God to be revealed. Could this be because up to that point the sons of God had chosen to remain hidden? What greater danger does the world face than to have neither salt to preserve nor light to guide? The Christian's greatest failure is to hide from the calling of Christ, for it is this person that God is using to bring His peace into a broken world through the message of salvation.

In Jesus' time there was overwhelming fear among the people because of things like Roman tyranny and a crisis of the identity of God's people. Christ came to restore his people to their rightful place as heirs to the riches of the Kingdom, and to be coheirs with Him. The problem He saw was always more deeply rooted in the spirit of man, and the problem was spiritual death, not physical, social, political or circumstantial concerns. When the world tried to shift the focus of Christ to the manifest issues such as disease, taxation, and oppression, Christ shifted its focus back to the disease and oppression of the human heart by addressing the heart's tendency to sin and that He was *the only way* for a person to be delivered from sin. Knowing man in his entirety, from the length of man's time on earth to what goes on in the deep recesses of his heart, Christ came to share the supreme insight of heaven into the recurring ailments of the world—this in itself would have been the most profound gift the world ever received. But He came to do even more than teach. He did not only come to tell us of the peril we faced, the resulting death, and the alternative righteous way for both Jew and Gentile, but to share in the things common to man, to die the death of the curse on our behalf so that we would not have to, under the condition that we put our faith in Christ completely.

With the knowledge of Christ and the gospel, a man is armed with the most terrifying truths to the dark powers and the most liberating truths in the universe. Apart from Christ man can do nothing, man can know nothing. All we can do is walk through life alienated from the Spirit of life, after which we may be picked up and thrown into the fire. We are useless from a spiritual standpoint. But it is precisely this selfishness which boasts the power of its own spiritual position and has learned to camouflage itself as normal and good within the world, degrading God's character into the confines of imagination and nullifying the power and importance of Christ's purpose and actions here on earth. This is the exposed position of man—the sinful condition conceals itself among its victims. This is why the life of the worldly person can appear so normal and inviting, even to the Christian, as though there is no reason to "bother someone with our religion." This is a trick of the devil to keep the gospel pacified, to keep the church paralyzed by neutrality and normality, so that he may maintain ownership of his people.

The less the church recognizes both the spiritual peril of the world, and the crucial position the church holds within the world, the more the church fades back into the pattern of the world. It is the church's humility that has permitted its survival to this day, and it is the pride of the church that makes God's name a byword among the people. It is the prideful church that often pretends humility and the humble church that at times appears prideful—like a bright, blinding morning light in the eyes of a world barely waking up from sleep. Of course it takes all day to allow the light to reach its fullness. In a similar manner, the church must put on the righteousness of Christ or be doomed to fail and lead the entire congregation into a false sense of security. The world that surrounds a church is destined to succumb to spiritual darkness and decay for as long as the church refuses to be salt and light. Light must be good, and it must shine in the darkness. The darkness cannot overcome the light if the light is indeed light. It must wake up the man who loves his sleep and who is comfortable in his darkness. It must make him aware that the darkness he was in was truly darkness and not actually light as he supposed. Anything less than total truth and total light coming directly from the presence and authority of Christ is the doom of humanity to meaninglessness and godlessness.

God knows what aspects of our character are ready to guide and what pieces of our old selves we are still clinging to. We do not always see it clearly. In fact, the more we boast our increasing ability to guide, the more likely it is that we are in no position to guide anyone at all. If we recognize our tendency to fail miserably and understand that we are unable to guide people to God without God's power, we may find ourselves more ready than ever. Christ understood this principle. He forfeited His entire will to His Father. Anything that is not from faith is sin, Paul teaches, and Christ was without sin so He could do nothing apart from faith. Apart from Him we can do nothing either, except fuel the fires of this world.

A LIGHT AT THE END OF THE TUNNEL

Every person, Christian or not, comes forth into the day, toils, eats his food, converses, and goes back to sleep when it is all over—only to wake up the next day and repeat the process. This pattern has set the many routes of civilization in its successes, failures, ambitions, achievements and abominations. These can all be found in the toil, food, conversation, and rest a person has. Civilization in its multiplicity of forms, nations and cultures are all driven by these and other aspects of the human machine. If we toil, eat, converse, or rest solely for a means to our own ends we are destined to impact the world pattern in a certain way. If we do these things to the glory of God and out of love for others we will impact the world in another way. As we do these things from either mindset, we work toward two common purposes which exist apart from ourselves. One is the fall and its later death brought about by human pride, the other is the resurrection and the life modeled by our author. One is dependent on our high opinion of ourselves, the other is dependent on recognizing the hopelessness of any spiritual progress apart from God.

There is a light at the end of the tunnel for both parties. Prideful man sees his end as the guiding light for the world, because he is his own god, and his way is what he considers to be the true path. This is the wide way which leads to destruction, the way set out by pioneers of discovering their own truth, an original path which has actually already been well-travelled, at least for some distance, by every human being who ever lived. These pioneers are less the first of their kind who are racing to be the first to at last discover something new, so that they can say "look, here is something new!" They are more pawns on a life size chess board, sacrificing themselves in the war against the enemy of their enemy. Every person to their detriment is recruited by the enemy and the father of lies. They are recruited by being told "look, here is something new!" But this new path has already been travelled many times, and the ambitions of those who walked it have already been tried and found wanting.

Nevertheless, we stand in the wake of thousands of years full of countless days lived by many men and women. Each person led a unique life in the physical for a common goal in the spiritual. Their goal was either to reject God and take their own path or to keep in step with the path of God's Spirit—there was no middle ground, although there was headway made toward understanding what the contrary path looked like. God wouldn't allow there to be infinite paths of neutrality so that we wouldn't be confused and so that we couldn't place blame on Him for the consequences brought about by our monistic rebellion, instead He called the path of this rebellion *one wide road*. However, His enemy neutralizes us by reinvigorating our sense of newness within the wide road and compelling us to consider the complexity of his countless and shifting ways. He is able to tear down Christians, or at least pacify them, and exalt many of his pawns to places of great honor, wealth and worldly renown. He unifies humanity under the banner of meaningless advancement and spiritual nullification—nihilistic striving—and disguises chaos as knowledge. This knowledge is nihilism because consciousness drifted from God who authored creation with intention and meaning. Therefore apart from knowing Him a man can know and do nothing. So knowing and doing nothing ironically has been a large factor in the construction and advancement of the whole of human civilization. Stripped from the meaning of the world's creator, creation loses adhesiveness. The human mind is a part of creation, and can be seen as an intermediary between flesh and spirit. The fully evolved, rationalist mind that rejects God is the decrepit, foolish mind in the eyes of God, whereas the mind of Christ is hidden in what appears foolish to the world. Postmodernism allows one to interpret all they see and hear to mean whatever they want, and to reject any interpretation they don't want as too simplistic. Those who follow postmodernism become re-creators of everything, in a sense, who try to make something out of unmade chaos in order to say "Look, here is something new!"

From the attitude of the enemy, who is the father of godlessness, comes many elements of Gnosticism, alternative religions (including cultural Christianity), and self-guiding philosophies. Many of these categories overlap one another. Each of them rests either on the anthropomorphizing or elimination of God, the rejection of Christ coming in the flesh, and the elevation of humanity to the status of gods—the fallen psychological condition of Adam and Eve and the social condition of the confused residents of Babel—both of which emerge from a spiritual disposition. The beginning of idolatry and its real-world impacts are some of the greatest mysteries we know because idolatry is the engine behind much more human activity than we are aware of. Idolatry is invisible to those who practice it, this is especially true in modernity, and apparent to those who avoid it. Those who scoff at the idea of idolatry are usually immersed in it, while those who see it as a spiritual plague can often read the signs of the times and draw past, present and future connections within the world pattern (these idols have taken part in shaping the world pattern). Those who can see the dangers of the world pattern can also identify what that pattern looks like, and those who long to adapt and live within the world pattern are unable to recognize its nature as a pattern at all. The only light they are able to see at the end of the tunnel is a light that already exists within the pattern. Nothing outside the pattern is visible from inside. From this pattern comes all forms of worldly knowledge that advertise themselves as transcendent but are typical. Human beings were created by and for their creator who exists outside of creation. Therefore nothing within all of creation can satisfy the deepest desires of the human spirit. The deepest desire is only for one thing, and it is by humanity's sinful desire that this one spiritual desire is synthesized with the world pattern in order to trick humanity into thinking that the need can be met by almost any other means.

There are two tunnels with two lights, one is the light of man and the other is the light of God. The light of man runs on manmade batteries, and can only illuminate the path for so long, and then the remainder of the path must be stumbled upon only by trusting those who have already travelled it. Its destination is only deeper darkness. The joy of this path is only temporary, even if it can be temporarily passionate or ecstatic (happiness). It can only bring satisfaction by feeding the pride of life. The life of man must be his own savior. He will only keep travelling the path as long as he can convince himself that it is a path worth travelling. Every time he falls down, he must be there to pick himself up—for he is alone on this path, as alone as everyone else who travels alongside him.

The second light is the light of God's righteousness, which the Proverbs tell us is like the first light of dawn, shining ever brighter until the full day sun. Think of it; walking on a path in the early morning is difficult before dawn. One will likely stumble or even veer from the path. They are beginning from the deep darkness. But as the morning progresses, we become more surefooted. It's not because we are particularly better at walking, but because we can actually see where we're going. So righteousness is not dependent on our efforts any more than walking during the day is dependent on a flashlight.

This contrast of light paints an unambiguous, black and white picture, like night and day, which may be upsetting to some, both Christian and non-Christian alike. For the Christian, they may see what I've written as extremely reductionist. I admit it may be, but I know no better way to describe the two lights I've experienced in my travelling along the two distinct paths. They may say that I have "tunnel vision." The non-Christian may see what I've written as incredibly biased and unfair to their position. They may see the path they travel as far more complex, enlightening, and beautiful than my narrow way of seeing it. I saw it that way as well when I travelled along it. But a road which leads nowhere must have convincing signs everywhere that it will lead somewhere. The catalyst to shift my own direction toward the "narrow way" was not personal enlightenment.

STOP SIGN

An act of obedience to the Spirit of God always requires a submission of our own will to God. This is disobedience to the flesh. A child who disobeys his father obeys himself. How then are the child's actions, which are obedience to his own law, considered disobedience in another weightier and realer sense? The answer remains embedded in a hierarchy of authority that is inseparable from creation and implicit in human design, although authority itself can become corrupt just like creation.

Good parents desire what's best for their child, not what's worse. What's best may include happiness and joy here on this earth, so the parents' desire for their child is not to rob the child of joy, but to preserve that joy in its truer, longer lasting form. The child may not be able to see this principle at work in the moment of a foolish action, perhaps because the forthcoming possibility of pain is clouded by a more immediate and fleeting joy. It takes a higher power—the parent—to recognize the danger within "misbehavior" and to turn the child in the other direction, which can be extremely painful for the child whose desire is brought to a sudden halt. Often this redirection of the child's momentum completely robs him of his immediate joy, but if this joy was leading to longer lasting pain (a broken arm, a trip to the dentist, a bad habit), the joy was futile anyway. The parents' correction protected the child from a larger pain by creating a smaller pain of contradiction or discipline.

The child may have felt severe pain brought about by the law (discipline). Likely this pain was a result of the child's wrongdoing being brought to his attention, so a realization of nakedness, vulnerability, embarrassment, and shame are a part of what initiates the pain. The child was previously unable to recognize his error. But the pain of discipline was about as temporary as the fleeting joy which would have led to a more permanent or intense form of pain. It took another who loved the child to see the pattern, to recognize that the child would not be able to see it, and to intervene so that he would be brought out of that pattern of behavior.

Human pride and arrogance result in prolonged pain and suffering. The love of others results in a deliverance from that pain. Love that delivers from pain is precipitated by admonishment. The earthly allusion to parenting is obvious, but profound. Just as certain dangers are imperceptible to a child but obvious to a parent, the spiritual dilemma that humanity faces is always certain and is impossible to discern without the help of "a higher power," the Holy Spirit's conviction of sin. Herein is a surface glance at the liberty of repentance.

The reason for our spiritual blindness to the circumstance in which we find ourselves is because of our ignorance of the horrible things that await us if we continue on the path we're on. But the path we're on feels so familiar and addictive that anything contradicting its direction is seen as evil in our earthly condition. This was one of the reasons for the cross, which displayed God's understanding of man's universal condition as subject to this blindness. The cross itself was a physical, political, and religious symbol of contradiction and centrality (though it was much more than a mere symbol). Two pieces of wood oppose each other, on which a man is hung who opposed the law of the land (a pagan law which in many ways opposed God). In Christ's case, God's only son, sinless and perfect, was crucified by man for contradicting humanity's sin at every turn and revealing the true nature of God to a people who thought they knew God. But what the world sees as contradictory, once viewed as an eternal stop sign, became the reconciliatory solution for the longstanding paradox of the knowledge of good and evil.

In light of the cross of Christ, the blindness of which I speak (which is really much more than blindness) is a condition that no human is exempt from. In fact, the more the person believes themselves to be exempt from it, the more likely it is that they are a product of it. The powerlessness of every person under sin is inescapable. Our childlikeness (folly) in the sense of disobedience must be acknowledged if we are to take the advice of the parent who can see the end result of our misbehavior more clearly, stop, and be restored to innocence and purity.

This is one of the most wonderful and terrifying puzzles of the Christian faith. For in one sense, Christ tells us that it is good, even mandatory to come to Him as a child, because it is the best way to display and understand faith; but in another sense God reveals to us that it is precisely because of our childish disobedience that we must come to Him. Disobedience leads to spiritual destruction.

The cross and the resurrection were clear signs of what truly brings life. Christ showed that the true joy and peace of the Kingdom in the midst of the worldly kingdoms would lead to the worldly kingdoms snuffing this truth out in whatever way possible; but those efforts were frustrated by the power of a Kingdom that cannot be presently touched, tasted, or observed—but is much more real than anything we can perceive with our physical senses. The cross showed what our world thought of the truth of Christ. The resurrection showed that the truth of Christ remains superior over the power of this world, even the reality of this world.

The cross is the spiritual stop sign that halts the world pattern. If we ignore it we continue on the path of life as our own saviors and at our own peril. If there was neither a universal human condition nor any spiritual danger which befell mankind, the cross would not exist. Neither would it if there was no God in existence in the only sense that He could exist. The resurrection is the assurance that the true journey begins only after we come to a complete stop. To reject Christ's revelation is to demonstrate the utmost ignorance of the human spirit brought about by pride. But it is worse than ignorance. It is a sign of lifelessness.

GREEN LIGHT

What is the acknowledgement of our lifelessness if not the first honest step towards true life, the life intended by our creator? After all, it is not the healthy that need a doctor but the sick, and it is not the living that need life but the dead. Those who are truly asleep do not know they are, but those who are awake know what sleep is. In the same way the dead do not know they are dead, but when they become alive they know that they were dead, and that they must continue to die to themselves every day if they are to live for God. The knowledge of the death that has been brought about by sin must be revealed to us by one who is able to see these things, as we can't. This is why the aroma of Christ and the Christian is life to those who live and death to those who are dead, but those who are alive were not made alive of their own will so that they could boast. The dead see God as the God of the dead, the living know that He is the God of the living, not of the dead, for their hope is in resurrection, not burial. Those who understand life to be only what can be found in the natural world and its carnal patterns are only able to find shadows of true objects. The eternal life that a person thirsts for comes only by the living water, just as we cannot live for long without water. Food and drink can be found in the natural world only as writings can be found of a writer. They are shadows of the real food and drink.

Even what is alive on earth is only a shadow of what truly is alive, for it is alive within a corruptible creation. The creature needs the creator in order to understand the true scale of its life as intended, which is incorruptible. The wages of sin are death, but the fruit of the Spirit are life and peace. One wage is a result of the toil of the curse. The other is a free gift so that no one can boast. The life of the Spirit is too lofty for us to comprehend. If we could comprehend these things we would boast about them. Who can't fathom the work they've already done or the wages that they've earned in their own strength? It is much more difficult to understand someone giving their hard earned wages freely to another who didn't deserve them.

Boasting is a natural inclination of the flesh, but it is unnatural to the Spirit. Boasting must be made visible to the world, but it is invisible to the Spirit—which is why

Paul, in the Spirit, asks "Where is boasting then?" (Romans 3:27). So boasting in our flesh is a sign of our sin, whereas boasting in Christ is a sign of our salvation. For if we can see only what we've made visible for ourselves, we are likely to boast about it to others, but if we see only what Christ has made manifest to us, we cannot boast of our work so as to undo what He has done. Humility is a sign of true life and true power because it was demonstrated by God, to whom we were blind in our pride. True power entered into human form, making Himself powerless before the wrath of God, changing the universal algorithm of what man is to be prideful about. Therefore, what the Christian is prideful about confuses and frustrates the world, because in the pure form of that pride the self must by nature be extracted, hidden from the world with Christ in God. Selfish pride in all its manifestations is a sign of ungodliness. Selfish pride, which is pride in the flesh, could not exist after the knowledge of the certain death it brought about.

It was the human heart that first carved idols in the image of men or of beasts, because the human heart had forgotten that it was carved out in the image of God. Turning from its source, the heart became malleable, reflective of demonic motivations and reflected in the now corrupted natural creation. Worship of God was traded for the next best thing, worship of the things His hands had made. Worship then devolved into the worship of the things which our hands made. We confused God's identity with our own.

Idolatry confuses the identity of God and proves that we know through the physical creation that He exists and that He always has, but that we are alienated from Him in our corruption. The person who boasts in what his or her hands have made—family, fortune, or fame—and denies the existence of God both participates in idolatry and collapses their own atheistic argument. For by boasting in futile things they participate in an act of worship. Participating in an act of worship proves they believe in spiritual meaning. Belief in spiritual meaning suggests an incorporeal component to reality and a spiritual source for spiritual meaning outside themselves. Who can be the source of the beginning, middle and end of all things, and who can bring meaning into all things? No matter how far one tries to escape from the truth to find what they think to be true life, they end up ignoring the reality of their alienated condition by suppressing and verifying a darkened understanding.

I make those suffering from this condition sound demonstrably stupid, but the truth is that I have proven myself to be equally stupid at one point or another. This is why the mystery of God is so appealing to man, yet His truth is so frustrating to man's flesh. His truth is as universal and inescapable as daylight. It's not inescapable in that we cannot reject it, just as we can choose to lock ourselves in a dark room to escape daylight. God is inescapable even farther than reality is inescapable.

Feeling sick is the first recognition of an illness, and visiting the doctor is the first step toward wellness. While ignoring symptoms of an injury or an illness can be a sign of one's physical "toughness," it can also lead to a worsening condition. Ignoring spiritual depravity and denying it's there can make us appear spiritually normal and "tough" to the world, even "divine," but it also increases our blindness to the growing danger of our condition as creatures spiritually alienated from the creator of our spirit. But so long as we fit in with others who are also under that same condition we can trick one another into a feeling of normality and community. The normality of sin is a paradox, for its universal condition is abject in the eyes of the creator. Retrospectively, it is the man of God who appears abject to the disjointed majority. We who are united with God are aliens living within the world pattern. The church is confusion and death to the secular world and a godless life is confusion and death to the church.

There has to be a red light before there can be a green light. A person must be stopped in order to start moving again. This is the gravitational nature of repentance, and it is contrary to what only acknowledges unhinged, upward mobility.

A.I.

In the 21st century, there is little room for paperback books, religious conversation, or genuine old-fashioned friendship. These things have become obsolete compared to their more advanced forms; paperback books have been traded in for handheld devices that hold the potential for unlimited, albeit filtered knowledge within them; religious conversation is seen as far less sensational than the "real world," which is often observed from behind a screen on *Netflix*, *Instagram*, *Facebook*, *Twitter*, or *YouTube* among other mediums; and old-fashioned friendship with a few close people pales in comparison to having an entire kingdom of internet followers worshiping your every move. Even sex has been replaced by its artifice, pornography—which is basically new age prostitution available without consequence (in a manner of speaking) to any man, woman or child with access to an internet search engine. In essence, mankind, in its newfound fear of "artificial intelligence" is coming to fear what is happening to its own intelligence—it is becoming artificial.

As a culture we are becoming fattened by so much "information" that we can no longer successfully navigate ideas because of intellectual obesity. Today we are seeing the costs of the emergence of a postmodern, secular, and pluralized culture. Society is largely bereft of true meaning due to the tyranny of sacrilege and relativism. These costs are amplified, not papered over, by modern technology.

Indeed, meaning is truly advertised wholesale to humanity in the 21st century, but it is more and more fleeting as it is cloned into yet another copy of a copy of a copy of meaning before a people who submitted to a redefinition of reality long ago. Again, we have been ensnared by the tools which were supposed to bring about the new man and woman and usher us into our next stage of evolution, just as the enlightenment and the industrial revolution were supposed to do. The industrial revolution brought about a massive increase in mankind's reach—toward riches, toward capabilities, and toward the heavens—and also brought about unprecedented fires of war, famine, poverty, and genocide which swept across continents, threatening the very survival of humanity itself. Today we have the intellectual version of this, and it is not brought about by

Google, or any particular system or philosophy, but things much deeper and darker than what can be built by human hands—our continued denial of the depravity of our own hearts, a rejection of the reality of human nature, and the consequence of unhinged human intelligence without God's loving foundation, grounding wisdom, or eternal truthfulness. Everything we see, touch, taste, and ponder is now interpreted through the lens of technocratic relativism. The judgment of God has been traded for the cyborg verdict of the human heart, a system of artificial justice to go alongside a young but evolving artificial worldview.

I could drone on all day about the technological and intellectual dilemma in which we find ourselves. What I mean by "intellectual" is the way in which we learn how to apply understanding of all the intricacies of the world pattern in order to reform and heighten the human experience for future generations. Utopia begins in the realm of ideas. It would be more fitting to recognize the presence of God behind all created things as we look at humanity and its developing tools. The spiritual and intellectual deficit that follows the worship of created things preserves and builds upon an ancient structure that has broken free from the shackles of the truth, the same truth who once presented Himself to Pilot.

The new system of roads is paved with gold and lithium. These roads wind throughout cities built higher than the builders of the first tower could ever fathom. They are travelled by cars which drive themselves with advanced GPS systems. At every turn there is a movie house, a bar, or a bowling alley—endless systems of entertainment and pleasure, with delicious foods that make our mouths water. As we drive along these roads, with our hands free of responsibility, we become bored, even in a city of endless possibilities. We become blind in a place where we were promised that we could see everything. The world of endless destinations has left us uncertain of where to go next. We truly drive on meandering roads of boundless length and possibility. There is only one problem. All these roads have are green lights.

PERPENDICULAR

The previous three chapters have dealt with three main things: there is something that keeps us going on the wide path of the world pattern; there is nothing in the world that can stop our momentum as we travel faster and faster in that direction; and a few of the new problems we face in the current technological age that amplify the noise of the world. I am not suggesting that anyone who is engaged with technology is more or less of a Christian or that they are sinning by scrolling on *Instagram*. The new forms of technology such as smart phones and social media are like a wheel or a match—material to be used as either a tool or an idol. Christ always speaks to us here and now, regardless of the items surrounding us in any given age.

Christ's words speak into the three problems discussed in the previous chapters just as easily as they spoke to 1st century dilemmas like taxation, Roman oppression of Jews, outside religion and philosophy, and matters of Jewish law—all of which sometimes coincided. The reality of Christ's life must be considered once it is made known. His teachings contradicted the way of the world as it was not meant to be. His death on the cross appeared at first to be the triumph of futility and ungodliness, but a closer look shows that Christ triumphed over sin. The cross is not something we can see, shrug our shoulders at, and then keep on driving toward the next helpful symbol that the world has to offer. Christ's resurrection is not another obliging philosophy or afterlife speculation, but the revelation of God's eternal life, the culmination of all His promises, and a blinding demonstration of His power. His life, teachings, miracles, death and resurrection were exactly the opposite of the world's view of itself. Christ troubled the world at every turn. His was the view from heaven of our world, yet in our world. These were the fulfilment of the promises made to our world for thousands of years. Christ's death and resurrection were the only way the incorruptible could permanently corrupt the corruptible so as to make it incorruptible again, tricking the world out of its helplessness and desperation.

The last thing the world needs is another helpful philosophy. Helpful philosophies come and go. They often come from corruption and humanity's profane desire to prevent itself from continued stumbling in the dark, without God's help of course. These philosophies which deny or manipulate the creator end up causing the world to stumble even more. They plunge humanity farther into the same condition philosophers are trying to heal. This is why Paul asks, "Where are the philosophers of this age?" (1 Corinthians 1:20). Their philosophies were nowhere to be seen as far as helping the human spirit was concerned. They were all overwhelmed by what happened to the son of God on a Roman torture device. They still are smashed to pieces by the empty tomb. So many philosophies view these two things as foolishness, as pipe dreams and fairytales. But these two things have something going for them that the explanations of the world do not, regardless of how foolish they sound to the world. *They happened* in order to reveal God's true nature to people in every age.

Many philosophies speak only to our corruptible, isolated and alienated nature apart from God. They assure us of their superior truthfulness and morality even as their authors often lived gross lives and descended into madness when they lived out their own philosophies. In short, they were puffed up and spoke many big words, but their words did not exist. They were mute and destructive to the world. They had no authority. They were sometimes set on fire by the pit. Their religions did not bring life. In some cases they brought unprecedented death and suffering.

The wisdom of the world saw the death of God's only Son as pointless. It still does. It sees Christ's life as a suicide mission and the sign on His cross as a suicide note. They cannot escape what the cross truly meant for them, or that the resurrection proved God was always wiser and stronger than men, even when He was humiliated in weakness by men. In other words, even if God acted rashly or foolishly or in an uncalculated manner—which I do not believe He did—at least He *acted,* which is more than the wisdom of the world can often say. In my opinion, this is part of why the Word of God is the Word made *flesh.* The Word made flesh is inseparable from the good deeds He speaks. His words and actions are one. He *is* the Word.

Jesus did not only see the problems of worldly knowledge apart from God, but often noted the hypocrisy of many of the leaders in Jewish thought and the teachers of the law. These were the highest intellectual authorities for the Jews at that time. He also rejected that some of them were children of the promise based on race alone. He noted that if these people were truly the children of Abraham, as they claimed, they would *do* the things Abraham did, instead of teaching and obeying human traditions. Many within the Jewish religious system were caught in a scheme of words and works without faith, and were cut off from the promise as a result.

The cross is the best philosophy to live by in this world precisely because it is not a philosophy at all, but an *act of love.* The act was finished within the world by the one through whom the world was made. And each individual when confronted by Christ's death for the forgiveness of sins mustn't see it as a philosophy with which they either agree or disagree. They must come to terms with its realism. Ask yourself, was Christ was a real person who lived and died as the four gospels say He did? And do His death and resurrection assure us of who He claimed to be without a shadow of a doubt? The "philosophy" of Christ is nothing less than a decisive binary choice dependent on His reality. In fact, Christ is the only lens through which we can accurately see the reality of things like science, ethics, history, and interpreting current events without distortion, for He was the one through whom and by whom all things were made, and all these things will be included in the redemption of the world. The Jewish focus was on the law and the scriptures, and apart from Christ they saw the scriptures through a veil. But Christ is the unveiling of truth for both Jew and Gentile. Apart from Christ we see the world through a veil. Our eyes are dimmed by the guilt and folly of sin. Apart from Him we see all things as coming from nothing but what we know and meaning nothing but what we want them to mean. No matter how eloquent our words are, apart from Him we can do nothing for Him.

The events of the gospel happened in a time and place far removed from us. This is a part of why the world has trouble believing. People say things like "If I could see and speak with Jesus now I would believe." Because Christ's life in the world is so far removed from us temporally, culturally, and geographically, we have trouble thinking of His actions as relevant to our present circumstances. Why should we abandon the immediate world pattern for something so foreign to what we know? Precisely for that reason.

Christ's teachings, His claims about His identity, and His sinless life were nothing less than shocking to a world that had been alienated from the true life God intended since it began. The Gospel still shocks people today, as it should. The only way it would have been the Gospel and advanced this far is if it also shocked those who heard it long ago, jolting them awake from a deep sleep. To the degree that knowledge of Christ changes our lives and to the degree that we start coming to terms with His reality, our lives are transformed, for better or worse. Even when we come to terms with His reality, it is not enough to grant us eternal life. There were plenty who knew who He was, even demons. There are many who are reasonably persuaded today, but who reject Christ because they love their sins. We must submit to Him, repent, and follow Him all our days, or we will perish. Knowledge about Christ apart from knowing the love of Christ means nothing.

THE CHURCH

I wrote this book, just as my other books, for the church *and* for those outside the church. After all, I never know who may pick it up and read it. It is not my job to judge those outside the church who participate in sin, for I myself am a sinner saved by God's grace. Sometimes it may come across that way. I'm only writing about the connections between scripture and modernity, namely the reality of sin, rebellion, and idolatry among other elements and how these relate to the pattern of the world and how the world sees things. There are reasons for unbelievers to recognize that sin is a spiritual phenomenon. This realization will help them, I hope, to understand that sin can only exist as a spiritual phenomenon if God also exists. God sets the standard, we fall short of that standard. If we set the standard, we'd only set the standard for sin by beginning from sin.

On the other hand, there is no reason for the church to dismiss the early writings of scripture as allegory, to diminish human sinfulness as a reality. Of course, I don't want to just talk about sin all the time without talking about hope. But many in the church preach hope without repentance, and it's killing the church and robbing the Gospel of its power. Christians still sin and need to know that they may be forgiven. But should we pretend that permitting sin to rule our lives because our world says sin is good will please God? Church leaders who talk about all the good things that God is going to do for us without talking about the fact that God owns us and wants us to do good for Him, not evil, is harming the church dramatically.

In 1 Corinthians among other epistles, Paul addresses the various problems of sin that were infiltrating the church. I'd say that all of these and more are popular in our churches. This is not an indictment for everyone. I want to write an encouragement. But it is rare, and considered hateful to expel someone who is consistently immoral from the modern church. The modern church has every negative thing described in the letters from the Apostles and Jesus, but at a level unseen before. This is not to say that if a man or woman sins, they should be expelled, or that we should consider all sins as equal in wickedness. But the church in general needs to take the problem of sin more seriously, and start believing again in the power and authority of scripture. Discrediting the authenticity of Genesis puts the church in spiritual peril.

For my part, I wish that I took sin more seriously when I first became a Christian. That's not to say I wish a brother condemned me every time I fell on my face, but for much of my walk I was unrepentant. Repentance was just a word. I hold no one else responsible for my backsliding. I returned to my own vomit. But God's love is slowly being transformed by the culture into an amorphous, arbitrary love where anything and everything is acceptable as long as we have a powerful church experience. I do believe God's patience is far greater than we know. But we shouldn't take His patience for granted and turn it into an excuse for sin.

Some Christians say that we should not thrust ourselves underneath legalism, and I'd agree. But I disagree with what so many describe as legalism. If a brother was caught up in drunkenness and I rebuked him, is that legalistic? What about sexual immorality? Homosexuality? Idolatry? Witchcraft? Drug addiction? Greed? Every book in the New Testament takes sin incredibly seriously. Why don't so many Christians today?

Christianity has become a religion, rather than a reality. It has become a series of traditions, practices, and beliefs that are advertised to increase church ranks, and the Gospel has become an opportunity for personal benefit. Many have shifted the Gospel to invite outsiders in for an incredible experience, a wonderful message, a personal word of knowledge, a mini miracle, a motivational speech, and an uplifting pat on the back.

Modern Christianity has forsaken quality for quantity. The success of the megachurch is often measured by the number of attendants. By that standard, my church is failing miserably. There are less than ten of us. Another standard of success is the net worth of the pastor, or the amount of income rolling into the church, rather than the power of the Holy Spirit to transform people's lives. I can't help but believe that God want's something different. Many churches believe that. We can't understand why our ministries almost never look like the Book of Acts. Perhaps it can't look just like that today. We are not the same as the Apostles. But many churches around the world that are forced to meet in secret and are persecuted report to have an experience of faith that seems to meet many of those standards of the Book of Acts. This is because so many martyrs and persecuted people are willing to lay down their lives for Christ and endure immense suffering. Many in the modern church are as well. And we all sin, even those in the persecuted church. But there is a clear distinction between a small church that meets secretly in a Chinese apartment to hide from the CCP and the modern American megachurch with a giant statue of the world behind it.

I have tremendous potential to shift from this understanding of the church to glorifying myself in pride and trying to make the church about my own vision of it. I am no less susceptible, nor do I think of myself as a reformer. I just can't look at scripture, and then look at the modern church without criticism. My criticism is affirmed when the American church compromises and turns a blind eye to certain practices that are completely barbaric and genocidal. Compromises like these are the reasons why Christianity is blamed for so many historical injustices.

It is my conclusion that the modern church is in serious trouble. I'm not able to fix it because I'm the problem. I'm too busy trying to rend my own heart before God.

COMING ALIVE

What makes you come alive? Is it the things of this life, things related to money, possessions, or reputation? I am sure that none of us necessarily bow to golden calves or have statues of Sidonian goddesses towering in our backyards. But each of us have our snares, our wooden idols so to speak. Apart from God there is no escaping the wide path to idolatry, for something must fill the void of our alienation from Him. And if we have to worship anything less than the creator, which includes the heavens and the earth as they are created, then we will only worship created things. This dooms us to futility in thought and life. All our deeds, when done in the presence of blind and mute idols make us as blind and mute as the idols we worship, even if we feel as though it makes us come alive momentarily. Perhaps it is the next commission paycheck, the next romantic partner, the next drink, or the next family activity. Paul warns that anything done apart from faith is sin—and Christ says that all things done apart from Him are nothing. So apart from faith in the Son of God we can do nothing but sin, even in the morally neutral activities, not because of what we do with our hands, but because of what we believe in our hearts.

In the new age the idols that continue to demand our sacrifices are extremely powerful, precisely because they are able to convince us that they are not actually idols, and that there are no such things as idols or idolatry—because in the new secular age, we are told that there is no God besides the god of our imagination, and therefore no worship, and therefore no false worship. The first step away from Christ is the first step into the presence of idols, and both Christ and His alternatives demand our lives. The idol demands that we sacrifice our lives and our children into its fires of futility and forsake the eternal life God has promised us, Christ demands that we forsake our lives in their futility and turn to follow Him so that we may find life eternal. Biblically and historically, when a person or a people first turn their backs to God, idolatry is soon to follow, and so is evil on a scale we did not think possible as human beings. This is because people turn from God, the author of righteousness and truth, and became blind to the binary spiritual nature of sin and goodness. Let's look at some examples: Adam and Eve's first thoughts which contradicted God's law led inevitably to the act of lawlessness, which was united with a lie from the enemy of God's righteousness, leading to exclusion from the truth and innocence which God intended for them, a permanent lawless condition; God warned Cain that *if* he did not do what was right, *then* sin is crouching at his door, so sin hinged on an act; the residents of Babel were so convinced they could know God from their own volition that they actually tried to storm the gates of heaven; the Israelites, when God was giving the law to Moses, impatiently built and bowed to an idol which their hands had made, for they did not believe in God's provision; the Israelites struggled with God and turned to idols for the rest of their lives, as God foretold Jacob when He wrestled with him and gave him the name Israel (struggles with God). All separate acts of rebellion against God are interwoven throughout time within the supreme human disorder.

Of course, one may say, we live in a different time and place than these ancient case studies. Why should we believe that we suffer under the same conditions as they did? The answer is hopelessly lost in the materialistic, evolutionary perspective, where all law and limitations are relative to any given individual at any given time. But if we consider the Christian paradigm, the pattern of this world makes a lot of sense. In fact it becomes the only thing that makes sense of simple evil, even as simple acts of evil were often the outworking of incredibly complex perspectives. Those apart from Christ see the evils that are present in the world, pain and suffering, somehow as objective proof that there is no God; yet they prove the existence of God when they abandon relativism to make an objective claim about the presence of evil or injustice, for God is the only one who can make sense of a consistent higher moral standard than the shifting whims of humanity. The pattern of the world illustrates again and again that turning from God will lead to a lifeless coming alive, a sensual worship of dead idols which in turn demand our death if we are to become as they are. There is no other lens through which to see the far reach, the failures, and the atrocities of humanity. Even if faith at first sounds mythological, it is well rooted in certainty—and the more we see things like the battle between good and evil through eyes of faith, the more the advancing nihilistic alternative which is only an outcropping of the chaos of sin fades into unreality.

Christ demonstrated a life unknown beforehand to humanity. He demonstrated the fullness of a life lived in perfect union with God. The plan God had for Christ's perfect life was to lead Him to the same death man had earned with his wages of corruption.

In Christ's life, teachings, and miracles we see the fullness of God and the fullness of man. For Christ, being fully God and fully man, transformed corruptible man in his disunion with God into incorruptible sons and daughters through His own righteousness, provided we live within total faith in Him from beginning to end, just as He is our beginning and our end—the Alpha and Omega.

In order for us to assume our new nature given to us through Christ and by Christ, He had to shoulder our old nature, putting it to death on the cross. Apart from Him we can do nothing, precisely because apart from Him everything in our old, sinful nature remains out of His blood that was shed for us and in our own circulatory system—so we are still alienated from the life of God.

This is the trouble of the gospel for the man in unbelief. For man in his unbelief cannot have the resurrection of Christ that he wants without the forgiveness of Christ that he needs, and he cannot recognize the power of the resurrection without acknowledging the need for Christ's forgiveness, or if he does not recognize the evil he's committed against God. Christ died for our sins and was raised for our justification, how then are we to be justified if we truly believe we bear no guilt or sin?

We are withering, even as we feel that we are flourishing: this is because we are only coming to what we perceive to be life through the things that are dead, and we attempt to approach incorruptibility through things that are in themselves corruptible. But if we come to life through the blood of Christ who lives always, we cannot ever die either.

Christ demonstrated first that it is death which is truly alien to creation, even though it is the only thing, other than birth, which is universal to all men and women. But even birth isn't universal as man wasn't born at first, but *made.* Death was not made, but was born from sin. Therefore death is what we all see as more permanent, even than life, for the mind of sinful man is death. But Christ, gaining the upper hand over death, revoked its promise and its permanence. He set those who were to believe in Him free from death altogether by His resurrection. This is why those who hope in His name can have nothing and die, as in the material poverty and martyrdom of the apostles, and yet have everything and live in eternal knowledge of the hope of Christ—which becomes within them a wellspring leading to eternal life. This hope, kept alive by the Spirit of God, grants humanity access to the tree that humanity was banned from and has desired from the beginning of the curse.

To know Christ as Lord is to be free from slavery to sin, which is born from a godless freedom. The first couple were enslaved to sin when they thought and acted apart from God. They were free only inasmuch as they were excluded from the Garden. Even so, as we live apart from God we are slaves in one sense and free in another.

Coming to life in all things that are of this world is only a shadow of what is truly intended by God. The shadow becomes our world, convincing us that it is all that there is, but the shadow of the world cannot be cast without the true light source and the true world. Our physical bodies are subject to decay and death only because they are shadows of true life. All that we see before us each day is only a shadow of the glory which could come of a day in union to the one who has given us the day. The manna in the desert, and our daily bread were and are only shadows of the true bread from heaven which was to come down to feed our spirits. The adult is only a shadow of the child who was closer to the truth because he had innocence and the power to believe.

Humanity has been educated by shadows. We have reached toward the heavens with all of our power and technology. We have conquered nations and founded unprecedented forms of knowledge. We scramble for the theory of everything which would by nature bar God from His own creation. We teach our children these values without values from an early age, forcing them to come to believe only in unbelief, and to submit their lives to a hollow pattern of meaning derived from sensuality. In opening our ears to all teachings apart from Christ, we have closed our ears to the truth. We have blinded ourselves by staring into the sun for answers. We have become voiceless as we've come to speak words without wisdom. We have strived for the things of God, and lost even the truest things of man. Satisfaction is draining quickly from all things under the sun.

THE DEATH OF DEATH

As the world passes away, we know that death also is passing away. For the Christian, death is foreign. It's not real. Death is the last lie, the last enemy to be overcome by life. Death is total darkness and it has visible dominion over the world. There is no human refutation of death. To refute it, one would need to experience it and overcome it. But to overcome it, one would also need to overcome the curse. To overcome the curse, one would also need to overcome sin. There is no overcoming sin in our own power.

God gives us our days on this earth without a constant obsession with death, or we'd be driven mad by the thought of something so hopeless. God has placed eternity in man's heart to point man to what's eternal. Man suppresses that eternity for what's fleeting and immediate, for what pleases the eye and is good for wisdom. This is often enough to fill our stomach, but never enough to fill our spirit. But the stomach will be destroyed by God. So our hunger is immediate and intense, and like death the pain of hunger feels eternal and final. But God chose the hunger of the body for bread to point to the eternal truth of the way to eternal life.

The light of dawn begins with one small gleam. Almost nothing can be seen besides darkness, but he who knows that the sun has risen the day before knows that the present darkness is passing away. And so each day is meant to tell us of Christ. His resurrection was the first gleam at the dawn of a new day, one that will shine eternal and never pass away. Death then, even as it intensifies in the world where it is granted temporary dominion, is like the deep darkness where nothing else can be seen. But the knowledge of the Christian, though he presently sees darkness, is overcome with an unshakeable and irrefutable hope. Shaking him free from this hope is like convincing someone that there never was day and that there never will be one again.

Even so, as the night is when we are asleep and the day is when we are awake, the age when death had been given authority over man will be long forgotten. So far this age is all we've ever known. When we fall asleep in Christ, in the twinkling of an eye we will waken from this age.

THE COMMAND

The Ten Commandments were not punishments for wrong living but strong and concise truths about moral reality and strictures that, if abandoned, would send a community into chaos. The first set of commands tell humanity how to respond to God and how to treat God. The second set of commands tell humanity how to respond to others and how to treat others. All these commands are summed up in two broader commandments—love God with all your heart, soul, strength and mind, and love your neighbor as yourself. Deviating from these commandments is a sign of spiritual death and causes the manifestation of suffering more than we know or understand.

The first set of commands speaks of what happens in our hearts when we forsake God, we create idols for ourselves to worship instead of Him. Modern idols are harder to identify, but the precept still holds strong that when God is devalued, another worthless thing (or thing that is worth less than God) is overvalued, even worshipped with all our heart, mind, soul, and strength. All of our efforts pour into something that is lifeless and temporary and our life in a sense become lifeless and temporary. God's eternality is traded for whatever this thing is and the lives of others are forgotten, even sacrificed at the altar of the lifeless and temporary idol, which is why the second, more visible set of commands follows the first, invisible set of commands—because the physical springs forth from the spiritual, and is secondary to the spiritual.

Just as death springs forth from a corrupted life, life must spring forth from fallible death, for death only lives and feeds on corruption and decay, which were initially bred by deception. Deception is in death's DNA. If God was life, then His commands would have to be life-giving—even to the point of putting those to death who'd transgressed certain commands. Even in modern society we put people to death who break certain laws *in order to preserve* the lives of others. We expel the wicked from among us. At the very least we lock them up for life.

Death came from disobeying God's one and only command. How much more will life come from obedience to another one of God's commands? When Christ visited Bethany to reassure his disciples that life has preeminence over death, He did not dismiss the pain, seriousness or finality of death, even though prior to His journey to Bethany He made death out to be nothing more than natural sleep. He understood that death was not to be underestimated, and He was troubled and deeply moved by the pain caused to the world by the death of the one He loved. He was moved even to tears. It was from this love of His friend that the command arose. And it was by obedience to this command that Lazarus arose. Of course, this miracle is the preface to Jesus's own resurrection which is of a different and eternal sort, itself a promise to those who follow Him that they will likewise rise from the dead. The command is life-giving and eternal, whereas disobedience is death-bringing and futile. To reject Christ is to disobey God's primary command, to receive Christ is to be liberated from bondage to decay.

It does us well to remember that creation itself was initially ordered by one command, that God spoke reality into its quantitative and visible form. It was only made visible by the primary command—"Let there be light" (Genesis 1:3). The promises of God throughout scripture are enriched by motifs of darkness being made visible by light, or light being shrouded by darkness. The primary command which was to order creation visibly was also a promise that death would be overcome by life. Jesus Christ demonstrated this hope throughout His life, through many miracles such as giving the blind man sight.

The Lazarus story, recorded in the book of John as Jesus's last public miracle prior to His own resurrection, shows a beautiful interaction between Christ and His disciples. He had almost been killed in the region that He intended to go back to in order to raise Lazarus. His disciples recognized an immediate danger in His return to that region. But Christ recognizes an even more immediate danger of not following God's commandments, which may lead us into worldly danger. He draws the analogy of the command that first ordered creation—day and night. He who walks by day will not stumble, but he who walks in darkness stumbles. In the world we can walk in darkness and be protected from what the world sees as death, whereas if we follow Christ we can be led directly into the world's traps, even into death itself, while knowing that death will be swallowed up by life. So the primary commandment which ordered creation—"Let there be light" (Genesis 1:3)—is also a prophecy that night would come and then day would come again. The Lazarus story proves that Jesus understood the connection between God's intentionality in structuring existence itself by the differentiation of day and night and the culmination of the new incorruptible heaven and earth first demonstrated by resurrection. All eternity and existence itself hinge on God's voice and our ability to hear his voice and respond to His command.

ONE LONG CHAPTER

It is difficult to open our eyes and ears today, regardless of beliefs, and conclude that there is no dilemma in the world. The 21st century has given way to an assault of ideas and technologies, resting on old foundations of the world pattern. It is wise for the church to recognize that "there is nothing new under the sun," (Ecclesiastes 1:9) and that what is not built on the foundation of the Word will fail. The world sees evil as a void concept today, so massive evils of the past are no longer present. But the existence and reality of evil rests on a spiritual understanding of the human condition, and is becoming impossible to ignore in the modern era. Scripture stands out in modernity with answers modernity cannot provide. But the church's compromising with modernity is diluting the power of the answers God provides. The church bowing to the whims of the world was also a first century occurrence. Christ modelled the wisdom and power of God to triumph over the wisdom and power of this world and to break us out of the prison of the futile worldly pattern. The worldly pattern in scripture was always entangled with idolatry.

Mankind in his arrogance forsook the immortal God and traded Him for false idols. This pride of life begins invisibly within the heart and moves outward into the visible realm. When our bodies, which include our eyes and ears, were abandoned as temples for the wisdom of God's Holy Spirit they became towers for the confusion of the world. Everything that came before our eyes was reformed as such, and therefore corrupted. Truly free existence within God's parameters is an ancient and foreign concept in the world, so anyone who finds it has found the only new thing in the world, that which is not of the world. When we are of the world we suffer because of the world and cause suffering in the world, and we die in the world unless we die to the world. So death which is unnatural, naturally became the most popular thing in the world. The idol therefore represents the shift in man's thinking from God to the world, life to death, wisdom to confusion, reality to its caricature. Everything was remade and redefined backwards. Nothing became the creator of everything. Humility was traded for pride. There can be no spiritual light in the world apart from the Spirit who created the world and the light who came into the world. Science has given us what we imagine the beginning and the end to be, but only God stands forever at both beginning and end.

When Jesus closed His spiritual parables with the words, "He who has ears to hear, let him hear," (Matthew 11:15), was he only preaching to those who weren't physically deaf? Not really. He was preaching to those who needed a way out. When our journey is fueled by pride and deceit it becomes impossible to be told that it is not a journey worth taking. Deceit and pride are what caused the heavens and the earth to begin decaying, to become corrupted, to become perverted. We sought to create the utopia of the new heavens and earth, but created a dystopian darkness. For everything in essence was nothing, life led only to death, and wisdom was traded for folly. Every generation is watching a world at the pinnacle of that confused state. The truth will waken us, whether in life or death. We have many paths to take today, and are told endlessly that every windy path is equal to another. These paths are formed by many people with passion, talent, intelligence and ambition, formed by vivid dreams and powerful desires. But the paths are still formed under the curse of the self. We are in the groupthink of self. God told us that we cannot save the world.

There was one gift at the beginning, the gift of life, but it was viewed in two different ways. Humanity's intention shifted from the will of God when humanity believed wrongly about His intention and will. But God's gift to us wasn't meant to exclude anything except evil. Choosing what we weren't meant to choose thrust us into the determinism of sin and spiritual blindness. We reformed the world to fit that determinism, therein lies the inescapable pattern. The gift became a wage, a sense of divine prerogative. True freedom could only come at a cost in the wrong sense, just as the Gospel brought true freedom by the cost of Jesus's righteous life being laid down for us. The gift of life became two different things, the first was reality and the second was a perversion of reality. Our freedom to choose at every point in life shows that life was a free gift, not a wage. Rejecting this fact leads to condemnation, which is why the wages of sin are death. The gift cannot be truly treasured as a gift without a restoration from the curse of death to the gift of life.

Our daily experience is overloaded with signs and slogans that emerge from the pattern of the world. Filling our minds with the things of the world is a way to gain worldly knowledge. In a way, it's a new aspect of information we are given when our eyes are open to what they aren't meant to be open to. We can gather that information and understand it in the same two ways that we understand the gift. Modern information is becoming shinier and more technological, even as it becomes more godless, in a way to make the much brighter and full life with Christ seem dull and uninviting. God has had to watch humanity fall into its own traps and then turn and blame Him for the traps they set for themselves for ages. The questioning of God brought about a flood of knowledge prior to the literal flood. The curse was God's spiritual judgement that preceded the physical judgement, just as sin emerged in the heart and resulted in the action. Humanity became the blasphemous judges of God and often lived their entire physical lives with this predisposition. At the end of their lives the judge was revealed.

The Tower of Babel was built out of this rebellion. It was not built from a neutral spiritual position but from a collective divine aggressiveness. Just as the individual thought gave rise to the individual action, the individual action gave rise to the collective action, the perpetual, universal revolution against God. The Babylonian disorder lies at the heart of every generation, the rise and fall of civilization. The acknowledgement of this disorder makes for extended national life, though there are exceptions. It's wise to consider that nations who reject God can be like a beautiful flower of the field, but will wither and be scorched by the sun. The utopian scramble dates back to the tower. We ought to see this as we manically construct things today. As we start building from the ground up, we often forget that the ground is cursed because of us, and is often cursed by the same ambition that drives us as we build from it.

I see the tower as a way for man to attempt an escape from the curse apart from the power and grace of God. This rebellion led to mass confusion and scattering. What happened at Babel was certainly a historical event, but it also has a longstanding allegorical significance. But the new age, being constructed on this same edifice is trying to reject that there is any intergenerational significance to the utopian scramble. But just as Adam and Eve's disobedience didn't come from a full understanding of why they must avoid what they chose, and the tower didn't come from an understanding that its construction was a deliberate act of rebellion, so the new age is being compiled from various ideas and notions that do not very much have God in mind, but are rebellious nonetheless. We all create fissures in the heavenly ceiling when we sin, even though we do not know it. Transgression is cunning in that regard. It says it's something new, but never is. The technological and informational boom give us an incredible look into this concept, as new things arise daily, but often only amplify the human condition through social media, blaring music, and advanced storytelling methods. These things give us the impression that we have the attributes of God. I wonder if the mighty tower that preceded the mass confusion of languages and scattering of nations had the same effect of intense awe and seduction on the people of that time.

Just as there is a similarity between the physical construction of the tower and the modern technological age, there is also a connection between the confusion that took place there and the confusion within the modern technological age. "Misinformation" is a common term today, and it is widely known that the internet and social media platforms can rapidly spread lies regardless of where the reader sees those lies as coming from. Just like Satan first deceived man and one man deceives another, the tools a man uses can broadcast deception in a revolutionary way, like an extremely loud speaker that cannot actually speak words with meaning. The modern tools are just another part of the pattern, albeit a very loud and persuasive part of the pattern. Regardless of the complexities of the broadcasted message, only two messages can be spiritually broadcasted. The persistence of these two messages show a consistent spiritual diagnosis and prescription. Recognizing the inescapability of the worldly pattern merits recognition of our entanglement within it. We are muted by it. We cannot tell others the way out without knowing it ourselves. Our words are lost unless they are united with the Word. Our words can lead others within the world but never outside the world. Speaking words apart from the Word shows that we want control over our own lives, that we think our lives are our own. But regardless of sheer influence, strength or intellect, our lives are not our own. We were bought with a price.

Even modern political paradigms recognize an inescapable dichotomy of vision. This contrast may be called the vision of the created eyes versus the vision of uncreated eyes. Both sets of eyes have contributed to the way the world is.

One is a vision that needs God and the other does not acknowledge God. One vision begins with the self and is prideful and the other begins with God and therefore must humble itself before Him. One claims to be new and vigorous but is old and dying, the other is eternal and life giving but is seen as restrictive, dated and constraining. Each civilization emerges from a sweeping vision that claims to see everything in one sense, but cannot see anything in another.

Each day begins and ends with a series of physical movements. These series of movements follow the dichotomy of vision. The sage of Ecclesiastes saw the accumulation of these movements as meaningless. We must admit there is a level of futility to the most grandiose gestures. The fall of man was the template for this burdensome task of investigating all the actions done under the sun. To us, who are always caught in these movements, the movements and actions of futility are seen as infinite and eternal, but they are always already passing away. The connection between the movement, the words and the visions that power the world's engine are so obvious a child can see it, and so it is scoffed at as overly simplistic.

A modern tool of the media to augment conformity is to discredit various people in certain areas of expertise. Those who investigate all the things that are visible to us are seen as the credible ones, and those who recognize the spiritual realities behind what's visible are dismissed as superstitious. This intellectual precept is similar to the worship of created things rather than the creator. It popularizes spiritual blindness. Man was granted dominion over the earth, but this dominion became flawed. The recognition of this flaw helps purify our dominion. All ancient cultures recognized the wrath of the gods as a looming threat, even if it was only seen as a stubborn philosophical precept. But creation itself cannot hold back man's ambition or evil tendencies. Realizing God's sovereignty as a philosophical truth helps quell the madness, but doesn't completely solve the problem.

The modern church's only religious problem is where it has forgotten the orphan and widow and allowed itself to be polluted by the world. The church is here to represent God in this world as the world slowly passes away, to point the world to the one who outlives it and who transcends it. Those who come to hear the gospel should not be simply given a different version of what the world has to say, but the Gospel. A world without salt and light will decay faster and fall into darkness. There are temporal fears among every generation, but Christ came to demonstrate an eternal hope to set us free from those fears. But this hope cannot be seen as long as the church resolves to keep it hidden. The church keeps the truth hidden from the world when it cannot recognize the presence of a lie in the world, which can only happen if the church is influenced by the lie of the world. The church apart from Christ can do nothing.

The laws and commands of God are not unconcerned with things like labor, conversation and food, because going after these things apart from God sets the world in its pattern. People can't build mighty towers without meals and good conversation. With God's light shining on the things we do, they are beautiful and not routine. Apart from God they are not from faith, and become polluted, sinful, and even nihilistic. Think of all the corporations that began humbly with a desire to help people, and became corrupt and greedy. If there's no God, corrupt people may never face judgement for what they do, so the fear of God helps ward off corruption. The fine line of reality has been formed by God to point humanity toward God and away from idols, towers of futility, and inebriating fruit. Christ didn't teach a multiplicity of paths, but two. One path is well lit at the beginning and obvious but ends in darkness, the other is like the first gleam of dawn, shining ever brighter until the noonday sun. Many will see my reduction of the various worldviews down to two dichotomous paths as unfair. But I was in no better position than anyone else travelling that wide road of paralyzing complexity.

If the highway systems in America allowed total freedom and autonomy, there would be mass chaos. People would be plummeting off of bridges and barreling into busy intersections. A child who grows up without discipline suffers spiritually more than a child who grows up with discipline. Even if the discipline hurt momentarily, the child's lifelong character was changed for the better. A red light is a momentary inconvenience but it saves us the larger inconvenience of being T-boned by a semi-truck. We often don't feel deep gratitude for the existence of red lights, but we do become angry at those who run them, even if they run them accidentally. In the same way, we often don't acknowledge the necessity of God's justice and the reality of His law or even His standards, but our hearts cry out for justice when His laws are transgressed. Whether someone lies to us, steals from us, murders us, or commits adultery, we recognize these things as moral wrongs in society. God has given us a major red light in the Gospel. The Gospel reveals that we commit all these transgressions not only against one another but against God, for whom the first set of commandments are written. Societies believe that we can scrap the commandments about God and keep the ones about our neighbors, but it never seems to work out well for us.

Is the Gospel only a red light? Of course not. The disciples did not celebrate the death of Christ, but His resurrection. The Gospel is foolishness to those who are perishing, but to those who are being saved it is the wisdom and power of God. We can only be saved and forgiven after we come to a complete stop. Then we may participate in the resurrection. Christ's command to the adulterous woman whom He did not condemn was to "go now and leave your life of sin" (John 8:11).

Today, genuine human experience is being traded for a simulated online experience that is advertised as more meaningful. It is simply more extreme, more intense. Could this be another trade-off of the genuine relationship between God and His creatures for the new, perverse way His creatures came to view Him once their eyes were open? Entertainment is ample today, but is meaning? Skyrocketing crime and suicide rates, world decay, Marxist revolutions, the destabilization of governments, the threat of totalitarianism, globalized infanticide, and the lack of human connection indicate that entertainment isn't the same as meaning, leftist solidarity isn't the same as God's righteousness and justice, and massive databases filled with information and computer generated algorithms aren't the same as wisdom.

There is an engine that fuels the world pattern and there is nothing in the world pattern that can stop it, for that would be self-defeating. Sometimes we think that a new philosophy or innovation or president or social movement or genetic mutation will be the catalyst to shake us free. The world almost never sees the cross of Christ as the solution. The world rejects the cross. The cross is a symbol of the world's rejection of God's son at the end of the ages. It is also a symbol of God's triumph over that rejection. The cross of Christ is therefore the best hope for the world because it is not a hope that is of the world or a hope that relies on a proper function of the world. The cross of Christ is far from our generation, yet it is always present, and always will be because it is true. The cross of Christ is shocking, and the only thing that can jolt us awake from our deep sleep.

The church cannot dismiss the relationship between God's Word and our modern age. The church's doubt of scripture deafens it to God's voice. Sin infiltrated the church in the first century, do we really think it can't do the same today? We can't trade God for the world's redefinition of Him. It is becoming less popular in the church to be set apart and more popular to be conformed to the pattern of the world. Christianity has come to see itself as a religion. Its success is so often measured by worldly standards—masses in attendance, production value and entertainment, weekly tithes. The problem starts with me. I often measure my own success in a similar way. To the degree I do this, I fail my own test, and contribute to the aberration of the church.

The reason that idolatry is the most serious sin, even prefacing the other sins in the Ten Commandments is because no matter what may be found on the wide road, idolatry is found there too, towering behind everything else. An idol is anything that takes the place of God. Do we really think advanced 21st century knowledge undoes the existence of idols? To the degree we do, we are unaware of the effects of idolatry and probably the most affected by it. Christ's life did not refute the reality of idolatry but offered a way to set us free from the carved images in our heart. It was the tree of death He had to carry up to a high place for us so that He could give us life. It was His final cry we had to hear for our deafness to be cured. We had to look upon the curse of our sin as it rest upon God's sinless son in order to be healed. These invisible truths trouble a world that believes it is innocent before God, even after it crucified God's son for shining a light directly into its darkness. It is common to see the world as flawed and corrupted and to forget to look at our own nature as individuals. But ignorance of the presence of sin in our lives is largely what keeps us in bondage to sin, like an abusive master who convinces his slave that he is looking out for the slave's best interest. Recognizing the damage of sin requires the Holy Spirit. Sin and the things of this world are vanity. Futility and grasping for the wind is meant to point us toward something real and eternal to hold on to. Only one person has visibly and historically reached out His hand to all of us and revealed a glimpse of life in a time without end. That person was, is, and always will be the Son of God.

In some respects, sin and death are all we've ever known. Yet their temporality remains hidden from us. Food and drink, day and night, nature and culture all point us to Christ's death and resurrection. Christ's death and resurrection give us hope of an eternal glory that dwarfs the only age we've ever known.

Human life is dependent on God's commandments, and the rejection of His commandments brings pain, suffering and death more than we can comprehend. His commands are binary—both physical and spiritual—but the physical is secondary to the spiritual. Deception brings corruption, corruption brings decay, and decay brings death—so death itself was given birth through deception. On the other hand, life is given through truth, and life has truth embedded in its DNA—truth is the way to life, and God is all three. God's commands, His prophecies, His existence, His incarnation, and His creation are all intertwined as the answer to "the human condition." Creation was ordered and structured by God's power and His commands, but His power and command were rooted in love, as Christ showed in the tears shed for Lazarus prior to His command to Lazarus to wake up from His sleep. Existence depends on our ability to hear God's voice and respond to His command. (Revelation 22:7).

ABOUT THE AUTHOR

Sam Wittke is a young writer who grew up in the Utah Mountains. His first two books The Best Guess and Big American Problems deal with Christian apologetics and the American political framework through a Christian lens. Wittke plans to continue writing books that inspire people for as long as he can.

Printed in the United States
by Baker & Taylor Publisher Services